The Sales Multiplier Formula

What do companies such as Northwestern Mutual Life, Hilton, and Nokia have in common? They approach selling differently than any of their competitors. Sales is not a transaction executed by the sales department; it's a process that all employees support. The result? The sale value for each new customer is most often double, triple, or even quadruple what their closest competitors achieve.

This book dives deeply into the exact formula for how you can achieve similar, if not even greater, results. Consider this your guide to shifting your organization from transactional selling to embracing a sales method that will explode your sales revenue, and engage your entire organization in doing so.

The reason for embracing this method extends beyond achieving explosive sales growth. The author has coached thousands of sales professionals over the years, and one challenge they face stands out more than any other. It's that selling is becoming increasingly difficult. Why do you think there are over one million sales-related vacancies in the United States at this very moment, according to the US Bureau of Labor Statistics?

Prospects are more challenging to reach than ever; work-from-home schedules, anti-spam legislation, and policies that restrict visitors are making it increasingly difficult for your sales team to do what you want them to do – sell.

Worse yet, when they do make a sale, it's as if they are burdening the rest of the organization. Complaints about unachievable delivery dates, unacceptable terms, or insufficient profit, all result in a clear divide between sales, and everyone else.

The result? A slow erosion of your sales, and an increased likelihood that your sales team will soon be searching for a different career. It's been this way for a while now, and it will continue to be unless you adopt what the author shares in this book.

The Sales Multiplier Formula

Simple Strategies to Multiply Your Sales by 4.68X

Shawn Casemore

Routledge
Taylor & Francis Group

A PRODUCTIVITY PRESS BOOK

First published 2025
by Routledge
605 Third Avenue, New York, NY 10158

and by Routledge
4 Park Square, Milton Park, Abingdon, Oxon, OX14 4RN

Routledge is an imprint of the Taylor & Francis Group, an informa business

ISBN: 978-1-032-73393-7 (hbk)
ISBN: 978-1-032-73391-3 (pbk)
ISBN: 978-1-003-50732-1 (ebk)

DOI: 10.4324/9781003463962

Typeset in Minion
by SPi Technologies India Pvt Ltd (Straive)

Contents

PART 1 Selling Is an Inside Job

PART 2   Your 4.68X Selling Opportunity

PART 3   Building Momentum with Your Sales Multiplier Formula

Foreword

It is the greatest time in history to be a customer, full stop. Never before have we had such a vast selection of options for the products and services we want or need. Moreover, the online tools we have for researching, connecting, purchasing, and delivering of the things we want, are more convenient than ever.

Conversely, it is a tough time to be in business. Competition is fierce, customer expectations are growing, finding and keeping good people is frustrating, and implementing new technologies is daunting.

This dramatically new business environment requires a profoundly different approach to selling as well. Think back just a generation ago. We would drive to an appliance store and have a floor salesperson explain to us the features and benefits of a refrigerator, or range stereo console. We would weigh the price and value and make a decision. If we wanted to compare, we would get back in our car and drive to another appliance store and listen to that salesperson explain why their appliances are better. We don't do that anymore. We don't have to. Today, we have the tools to learn everything we want before ever engaging with a sales professional.

The role of the salesperson has changed. Today, the discussion is less about the quality of the product or service (that has likely been well established) and more about the availability of stock, flexibility of the terms, speed of delivery, quality of the engagement, and preferability of the experience. Sales today is less about whether you are a good choice, but rather why you are a better choice than the other available good choices.

In the pages of this marvelous book, Shawn Casemore makes a compelling case for why people buy today. Online portals have made transactional sales quick and simple, but relational sales requires both fresh and more effective approach than so many outdated strategies. Shawn recognizes that it's rarely a single individual that takes a prospect from interest all the way to purchase, but rather a strategically orchestrated team approach that directly or indirectly contributes to the exposure, introduction, education, relationship, and sale. As they say: "When you see a turtle on a fencepost, you know it didn't get there on its own."

My work is in helping companies enhance their customers' experience by taking the necessary steps to become "ridiculously easy to do business with." The challenge today is that everyone is good – or good enough. And sometimes, good enough at a better price point is a better choice. That's why Shawn Casemore's insightful strategies and actionable sales tactics in this book are so needed today. Others offer "timeless" strategies that have become outdated. I submit that "timely" approaches are needed to capitalize on the new opportunities this rapidly changing business environment is creating. This book provides that.

Finally, forget what your teachers told you in school and write all over this book. Highlight passages, dog-ear pages, and write in the margins. It's not a library book! It's your book and I promise there will be passages you will want to remember and revisit. And when you find profound words of wisdom – which you will come across frequently in this book – share them in a social media post! Just give credit to Shawn Casemore.

David Avrin, author of *Ridiculously Easy to Do Business With – A Practical Guide to Giving Customers What They Want – How and When They Want It.*

Acknowledgments

To my wife Julie, who has always been supportive of everything I do, even if she doesn't fully understand why I do it. To my boys, who inspire me to work harder and be a better father and person.

My thanks to Michael Sinocchi, Publisher at Taylor and Francis. Without his support, this book (and two others before it!) wouldn't exist.

Lastly, thank you to all my clients for your continued belief in my work, and your willingness to try new things. Your unwavering confidence and support fuel me to continue digging and sharing new insights and opportunities to increase your sales.

About the Author

Shawn Casemore is a keynote speaker, sales coach, and advisor. He is the Owner and Founder of Casemore and Co Inc., a global consulting firm, and has worked with organizations such as CN Rail, Tim Hortons, Pepsi Co, MNP, Bank of Montreal, and over 200 other leading organizations.

His speaking typically includes over three dozen keynotes each year at major conferences, as well as speaking at sales kick-off meetings for major corporations.

Shawn's publishing includes 100s of articles in print and online for publications such as *Forbes*, *Fast Company*, *Chief Executive*, *IndustryWeek*, and *The Globe and Mail*. He's also written four commercially published books, including his most recent, *The Unstoppable Sales Machine* (Taylor and Francis, 2022) and *The Unstoppable Sales Team* (Taylor and Francis, 2023).

To learn more about Shawn and his work, or to arrange to have him speak at your next event, visit www.shawncasemore.com.

Introduction

When I sold cars in my twenties, my rapid success wasn't the result of studying sales strategies gleaned from watching VCR tapes on how to sell cars (yes, I'm that old). Instead, it came from the methods I deployed to upsell, cross-sell, and gain referrals from every prospect and new customer I encountered. These strategies, coupled with the relationships I built internally and externally with the dealership, combined to multiply my sales faster and more consistently than any other sales agent: the relationship I built with the service manager and service advisor, whom I introduced to my prospective customers and who returned the favor when asked about who to speak with in sales; the relationship I built with Finance, who knew what to offer a new customer to enhance their investment (i.e., undercoating, extended warranty) and in turn who referred friends and connections to ask for me when they arrived at the dealership.

Back then, I multiplied my sales by applying three rules that are still relevant today:

1. Sales is not an independent venture but a team sport that engages others in your mission.
2. Every customer or client is only satisfied when they have a complete understanding of the options, features, and complementary products that will enhance their purchase.
3. A systematic approach to approaching every prospect and customer is the only way to ensure you maximize the relationship and the resulting sales.

You might think that some of these strategies, first learned over 25 years ago, would be irrelevant today. They're not. Isolation caused by hybrid work schedules, increased use of digital tools for team communication, and a drive for improved departmental efficiencies have created barriers within companies that directly influence sales. It isn't easy to sell as a team, share the various options and features, and maximize sales revenue when you don't have a supportive team, precise offers, and a systemized way to present such.

Fortunately, there is a solution, one that I lay out in extensive detail in this book. The title aptly describes the outcome of your efforts. So, if you're ready for explosive sales growth and you're open to learning what other top-performing companies are doing to achieve a 4.68× multiplier on their new sales, then let's dig in.

Shawn Casemore
Chatsworth, ON
April 2024

Part 1

Selling Is an Inside Job

Selling is becoming increasingly difficult to execute in isolation.

Prospects are more challenging to reach, decisions involve more people, and expectations for customized solutions have become the norm. To make matters worse, employees who aren't in sales often don't see the need to be involved, making long-term customer relationships (and the ability to capitalize on those relationships) a challenge.

Fortunately, there is a strategy you can easily deploy that will multiply your sales AND engage the entire organization in the effort.

DOI: 10.4324/9781003463962-1

1

How Your Customers' Buy Has Changed

Take a moment to consider how you purchase products for your life today. Most likely you spend much of it researching online, speaking to colleagues and peers for their opinion or referral, and looking for options that best suit your intended outcomes. Well, these simple shifts are also impacting how companies buy your products and services.

THE BIGGEST ASSUMPTION IN SELLING

My unofficial exposure to selling came at the tender age of 11. After repeatedly asking my parents for a new BMX bicycle, they suggested I needed to earn money if I had such expensive taste. My neighborhood friend John had just acquired his brand-new BMX from his parents, and as someone who spent a lot of time riding my bike and exploring our neighborhood, I was jealous. Maybe it was the bright green paint, the hand brakes, or the knobby tires that captured my attention, or it could have been that my old red bicycle, with a torn banana seat and less impressive tires, just seemed old and outdated. Regardless, I was convinced that if John deserved a new bike, so did I. My parents disagreed at the time, and unfortunately, I didn't replace my red bike that summer, although there was an exciting surprise waiting under the Christmas tree for me later that year.

Determined to take matters into my own hands and never again be faced with wanting something my parents were not ready to buy for me, I began asking to do odd jobs around our house to earn an allowance. Let me be clear: I did not have a difficult upbringing, and my parents have always been supportive. My parents, having grown up on a farm in the late 1950s and early 1960s, believed that you needed to earn things to have a greater appreciation for them, a philosophy my wife and I continue to encourage for our two boys today.

My odd jobs around our house expanded to include mowing our lawn that year, and it was only a short period before our next-door neighbor, who spent most of their summer away at their cottage, asked if I would mind mowing their lawn. In return, they offered me ten dollars, equal to my entire week's income from chores. Excited for the opportunity, I leaped at the chance and launched my little lawn-mowing enterprise that summer. My little enterprise grew, however, with minimal effort on my part. Neighbors throughout our neighborhood began observing me mowing lawns. They'd inquire about my services, and soon, I had acquired several additional lawns to cut. My parents, who were always supportive, encouraged my new business venture.

As the summer rolled on, I wondered how I might earn even more money from my little business venture. I shared my desire for more clients with my existing clients, who began introducing me to other neighbors they knew. However, only some were interested in having their lawns cut. As a result, I started offering my clients additional "complimentary" services as neighbors, including help with their gardening, staining their fences and decks, and even washing their cars. In the winter months, I transitioned to shoveling snow from driveways and rooves and even did some babysitting.

Although my exposure to sales at this young age may not have been overly challenging, it did provide me with some insights about selling that I still carry with me today. One of these is essential to share with you if your role or priority is to increase sales revenue for your company.

The purpose of an initial sale is to solidify additional selling opportunities that far exceed the value of the initial sale.

In other words, the first sale made to any new customer should be considered a gateway to additional selling opportunities that, if positioned correctly, can dramatically increase each unique customer's revenue.

Many business owners, executives, sales leaders, or sales teams I interact with today assume that closing the initial sale to a new customer is the greatest challenge. We invest so much time, energy, and money into prospecting and closing an initial sale that we often need to consider what comes next.

Just look at any sales department, and you'll likely find that once an initial sale is made, customers are transitioned to customer service or inside sales to "take care of things." Sales then move on to their next prospect to close another new sale.

Reflecting on my first entrepreneurial venture, I realize my sales didn't grow because I constantly focused on finding my next customer. Instead, I increased my sales by growing each client account and then capitalizing on the success of each account. In other words, by introducing new "complimentary" services and offerings, I was able to grow each client account in terms of revenue and selling opportunities, building more robust and more positive relationships with my clients, who, in turn, introduced me to their network of other potential clients.

If you believe that making the initial sale is your priority, and your goal is to multiply your sales, then you need to shift away from focusing much of your time and effort on the "next sale." This perspective limits your ability to make additional sales that could double, if not quadruple, your existing sales revenue without ever having to prospect or pursue a new customer or client again.

Have I gained your attention?

After working with hundreds of organizations, from banks to distributors, recruitment firms to insurance companies, and SaaS companies to manufacturers, even not-for-profits, I can unequivocally say that for every sale you make, there are additional selling opportunities that can increase your overall sales value by up to 4.68 times. I'll explain the ".68" shortly, but for now, know that you have significant opportunities to multiply your sales.

In other words, for each selling opportunity you generate today, you can capture many additional opportunities with little to no effort on your behalf. Most importantly, these opportunities don't require hiring more people or investing in new technology.

Is this something worth pursuing?

Before we go any further, let me explain why you're likely unaware of or not fully capitalizing on this opportunity today. After working with hundreds of organizations around the globe, I've found these to be the biggest mistakes most companies make when multiplying their sales. Take a minute to review this list and reflect on whether any of these apply to your company.

REASONS WHY YOUR COMPANY ISN'T MULTIPLYING SALES TODAY

- You only have a single product or service that you sell.
- You don't provide your buyer with options.
- Your sales focus is heavily weighted toward closing new prospects.
- Customers or clients don't recognize other ways you can assist them.
- You are known for one core product or service, nothing else.
- Existing accounts are transitioned to customer service or inside sales to "manage."
- You haven't developed upsell options to complement your main product(s) or service(s).
- The life cycle of your product or service is lengthy.
- Referrals are not a primary focus of your sales strategy.
- Your sales compensation or rewards do not reward additional sales.
- Quotes or proposals are highly technical and provide a single selection.

Does any of this sound familiar? You may have tried to launch a new product or service, but it didn't gain traction with your customers. Possibly, you expect the sales team to ask for referrals regularly, but they need to be more successful in attaining them. Or what you sell is highly technical or complex, and you don't believe the sale allows for additional options or features.

If any of these perspectives sound familiar, you need to take advantage of a massive selling opportunity, and the chance to increase the size of each customer or client account you have today.

TODAY'S CUSTOMERS: FICKLE, FIDGETY, AND FRUGAL

For years, studies have suggested what we already intuitively know about today's customers. Consider your behaviors and expectations of the people and companies you buy from. Today's customers want what they want, when they want it, at a price that they perceive to be reasonable.

Some additional nuances relative to customers have evolved in recent years, particularly since the COVID-19 pandemic, further influencing buying behaviors. A study conducted by Demand Gen[1] highlights several trends that have shifted substantially in recent years, most notably:

- 59% of all buying decisions involve three or more people.
- 56% of B2B buyers seek information that speaks directly to and demonstrates expertise around the needs of their industry.
- 68% of buyers choose a vendor based on a "knowledge of our company and its needs."
- Aside from price, 56% of prospects value what other customers say about a company more than what the company has to say about itself.

What's most important to take away from this study is that customers today expect the product or service they buy and the experience that leads up to and follows that investment to be highly customized and directly relevant to their specific circumstances.

This study, and others like it, sheds light on several new considerations we must make regarding influencing our customers to buy, namely:

1. More people are involved in buying decisions, so the days of focusing solely on a "decision-maker" and ignoring the possible "decision influencers" are gone.
2. Customers seek companies who fully understand their needs and provide solutions (products and services) that satisfy them.
3. Making a sale requires providing solutions that consist of various options that address customer challenges or objectives, thereby creating the perception of customization.
4. The experience your customers have of your company before, during, and after the sale determines the extent to which you can upsell, cross-sell, and resell them.
5. Capturing the attention and commitment of today's customers requires the support, input, and involvement of employees outside of the sales department.

When you consider these shifts, it becomes evident that selling can no longer be left solely in the hands of your sales department. If you want to capture new customers, close recent sales, upsell, gain referrals, and cross-sell, it will require everyone in your company to be supportive of and involved in selling, regardless of its size. Gone are the days of expecting sales to work their magic and everyone else can sit back and wait. Selling today requires a sales strategy encompassing all departments that directly and indirectly influence sales.

Unfortunately, these evolving customer demands and increased expectations come when most companies need help finding and retaining good salespeople. In other words, there is an increasing dichotomy between what customers expect and what companies provide. To compensate, companies are outsourcing their sales, introducing new technology, and relying on marketing to produce customers who are ready and eager to buy. Unfortunately, all of these "solutions" (which is what the companies selling these suggest they are) are resulting in more problems than they solve, for example, an over-reliance on technology to handle the sale, a lesser focus on servicing customers, expecting they can serve themselves, and so on.

You may have experienced this diminishing focus on selling firsthand, for example:

- You visit a new retail store to check out its merchandise, and while browsing, employees ignore you.
- You stop by an automotive repair shop and patiently wait for someone to help you, leaving after a few minutes of not being acknowledged.
- You call to book a reservation at a restaurant, only to be placed on hold and disconnected.
- You call a roofing company to ask for a quote for new shingles and are told an estimate over the phone (without anyone ever offering to come to your house to look at your roof!).

Unfortunately, many customers who decide not to move forward with buying your products or services or who limit their investment in your products or services aren't prominent. In other words, you're losing customers and sales that you didn't even know you had in the first place. I call this the *Lost Sale Opportunity*.

Figure 1.1 identifies how the *Lost Sale Opportunity* can quickly accelerate.

FIGURE 1.1
Lost Sale Opportunity (matrix with severity left and cost bottom)

DEALING WITH UNREALISTIC CUSTOMER EXPECTATIONS

With growing demands for personalization and an experience to match, it might seem impossible to satisfy and sell to today's customers. The answer, however, lies within the challenge. To fulfill what may appear to be increasingly unrealistic expectations of today's customers, we need to focus on *how we sell versus what we sell*. In other words, continuously customizing our products or services to satisfy a broadening demand by our customers is not the answer.

Instead, we must focus on selling fewer products or services while providing more options and variations in how customers or clients experience these products. Let me repeat this because it's an essential distinction that today's top-performing sales professionals recognize that others don't. When customers increase their demands for more personalization, it's often interpreted (by organizations) as customization. The phrase "customize or die," for example, is designed to justify why a company might attempt to develop, launch, and consistently sell many different products or services.

I've long been a fan of Apple products, a company that focuses on consistently offering new versions of their products. Although a fan, I have not found any significant advantages or value in upgrading to the latest iPhone. What would add value is the different options for holding the phone in various environments. A product that would allow me to mount my iPhone in my car or carry it without having it in my back pocket. Sure, there are plenty of aftermarket products for this, but they are all different from Apple products. In other words, fewer product iterations and more options would entice me to invest more heavily in Apple.

The drive to satisfy today's customer creates several significant problems, all of which impact your ability to sell:

1. The costs of consistently developing, testing, and launching customized products or services are extremely high.
2. Developing and delivering a growing library of products or services requires more internal expertise, which means hiring more people with specialized knowledge or experience.
3. Monitoring and ensuring a high level of quality in every product or service lessens as the number of such products or services increases.
4. A wider breadth of products or services makes it increasingly difficult to measure the margins and overall profitability of those products or services.
5. The sales team, faced with a growing list of products or services to sell, must be more educated (and therefore less comfortable) with the value each product or service can provide, which in turn lessens their ability to sell those products and services effectively.

There's an old saying, "We can't be all things to all people." Suppose we expect a sales team to sell. In that case, they will need, among other things, a clear understanding of the product or service they will be selling, its features, functionality, and most importantly, the value it can provide a new customer. Without these, the salesperson lacks the knowledge and, more importantly, the confidence to sell.

When faced with a growing number of products or services to sell, many sales professionals will default to selling the products or services they know and feel comfortable with while ignoring the rest. I call this *Comfort Selling.*

Comfort Selling results from our natural tendency to take the Path of Least Resistance, choosing the easiest way to do something rather than the best way. Unless a prospect or customer asks for a new or different product, a sales professional will tend to share or present the exact solutions they have offered in the past that resulted in their closing the deal, staying within their comfort zone. Abraham Maslow once said, "If the only tool you have is a hammer, you tend to see every problem as a nail."

What do you think most companies tend to do when faced with sales professionals practicing comfort selling? They introduce *even more* products or services for their team to sell, assuming what they have introduced for products or services that aren't selling was a mistake on the part of engineering or product development.

When sales professionals fall into the trap of comfort selling, pressures to sell products or services that aren't moving increase. This can result in sales making promises to customers beyond what their organization can reasonably deliver. In other words, rather than defaulting to different products or services a customer might be interested in, sales professionals begin to "customize" what they are already comfortable with.

STORIES FROM THE SALES FLOOR

When I sold cars in my early twenties, a new model called the Pontiac Vibe arrived.[2] The model was unique, and I was one of two salespeople who had the privilege of attending an event where the car was introduced, including a full explanation of all its features (and benefits). Soon after returning to the dealership, I sold my first Pontiac Vibe (the first salesperson at our dealership to do so). After this, many of the senior salespeople, who had more experience selling Buick's and GMC Trucks which the dealership had carried for years, would introduce me to any customer they met interested in a Pontiac Vibe.

Despite the opportunity to sell a new product that I'd proven was in demand, virtually all the other sales agents stayed within their comfort zone, choosing to sell products they were familiar with (and therefore more comfortable with) and turning over the opportunity to sell the new product to me.

Offering custom solutions that extend beyond one's comfort zone can be seen everywhere, from professional services firms to companies that sell products. Professional services firms such as accounting firms, legal firms, recruitment firms, and even investment firms might make promises to satisfy their clients even though they cannot satisfy the promises, for example:

- An accounting firm of CPAs agrees to assist with an acquisition without having the previous skills or specialized ability to do so.
- A legal firm agrees to help its client who is launching a franchise without having the specialized knowledge or experience.
- A recruitment firm specializing in recruiting senior executives agrees to assist their clients in finding skilled trades without having the networking or connections to make this happen efficiently or effectively.

Companies that sell products can fall into the same trap. Explained as a focus on continuous "innovation[3]," these companies develop and launch new products without first ensuring significant demand for them and before removing other lower-performing products from their line. They expect their sales team to become experts in every product's unique distinction. The result, however, is that sales most often introduce customized solutions built on products they are comfortable selling.

Here are some examples:

- A distributor takes on a new line of products that is different than what they have been selling, then expects their sales team to generate sales without a clear understanding of whether the product line is something their buyers seek.
- A customer asks a bakery product reseller to begin selling a new candy line, and sellers are expected to generate new sales within three months, even though their contacts are primarily in different departments.
- A manufacturer who produces specialized hardware decides to offer our machining services with existing equipment capacity and expects their sales team to "sell" the new service to existing customers without ever confirming whether there is a need.

My point is this. Having more to sell doesn't equate to selling more. Quite often, this results in the exact opposite outcome.

WHY SELLING LESS EQUATES TO SELLING MORE?

If increasing the breadth of products or services you offer your customers to satisfy the growing demand for customization isn't the answer, then what is?

First, let's clarify something. You can add more products or services to your offerings for customers or clients; however, you must be strategic. You should take six steps to ensure the sales team fully embraces any new product or service you introduce and, in turn, is something they discuss, present, and sell to your customers.

SHAWN'S METHOD FOR INTRODUCING NEW PRODUCTS OR SERVICES

1. Involve sales in the identification of potential new products or services. Sales represent the customer and often have a direct line to existing and potential customers. As such, they should be involved in discussions about identifying a new product or service.
2. Include "sales research" as well as "market research." Many companies will invest in market research to confirm demand for a potential product or service. Although this information can be helpful, it must often be more specific and accurate, leading to assumptions made without involving sales to validate their findings or observations. Make sure sales provide their own "research" to support your decision-making.
3. Sales test new products or services. The best way to validate demand is to have a select group from your sales team discuss the new product or service with your existing customers. The easiest method is to use one-to-one discussions or smaller focus groups. Doing so will validate potential demand and allow sales to become "comfortable" presenting the product or service in a safe environment (i.e., no sales targets to meet).
4. Have sales contribute to the product or service launch. In many instances, a new product or service launch involves presenting it to sales and explaining why it's so great, handing them some brochures

and a sample, and expecting sales to result. Instead, have vital members of your sales team involved in the launch, sharing their insights and observations with peers and discussing the language and best methods they've found (from step 3 above) for introducing the product or service to customers.

You capitalize on several advantages by taking a more sales-centric approach to identifying, launching, and introducing new products or services, ensuring increased sales. Additionally, you avoid wasting time and investment on products and services that don't meet your customers' customization demands.

Here are just a few examples of the additional benefits you'll achieve using a sales-centric approach to product or service development:

- You increase the sales team's engagement in the launch process, improving your ability to generate more sales.
- Customer or client feedback on interest and uptake is understood *before* introducing the product or service.
- Excitement is generated among the sales team to learn about and start sharing the new product or service with their customers or clients.
- Input from sales on market interest and uptake is identified before launch, enabling improvements to the product or service to ensure a successful launch.
- Improvements to the product or service are identified before launch.

My clients who use a sales-centric approach develop fewer products or services but enjoy a continued increase in sales.

More importantly, by increasing sales involvement in the development process, comfort selling is minimized, which increases the ability and willingness of salespeople to launch products or services that align with what customers want.

Henry Ford's[4] co-written autobiography, *My Life and Work*, published in 1922. He describes a meeting in 1909 with his company's salespeople, who wanted him to add even more models to the company's lineup. Instead, he announced he would build only one, "*I remarked: 'Any customer can have a car painted any color that he wants so long as it is black.'*"

Ford's bold statement makes sense when there is little competition to contend with and high demand for the product (or service) you sell. Tesla, an automobile manufacturer, was able to make and apply similar claims to the production of its first vehicles, the Roadster and its Model S[5].

Well, it isn't 1909, and it's fair to say that your company likely isn't Tesla.

Most companies need a customer base clambering for their product or service *before* also wanting some degree of customization of that product or service to suit their unique situation further. A study by Deloitte[6] suggests that 50% express interest in purchasing customized products or services; however, walking down the cereal aisle of any grocery store, noting the number of different brands of Cheerios or Shreddies, and it's evident customization is necessary to meet the growing demands for customization by today's customers.

Ford and Tesla both recognize what most executives and business owners do: simplicity of offerings leads to efficiency and, therefore, profitability in sales. The pursuit of personalization likely means you'll need to launch new customized products and services continuously, reducing operational efficiencies, eliminating opportunities to achieve economies of scale, and overwhelming your sales team to the point they default to selling for comfort, not for the customer.

We're left with a simple question: How can we create a customized customer experience without increasing costs? Can we further customize our customers' experience and improve our sales and profitability?

Fortunately, the answer lies in creating more awareness and engagement in sales. Something I refer to later in this book as Team-Based Selling.

Blinds to Go is an excellent example of a company that places sales at the forefront of its mission. Even as someone looking from the outside, their focus on growth is evident. If you visit their website to inquire about a career, you'll read "*Growth, ownership, and leadership. Join our winning teams, composed of individuals who share our values and passion for building a great company*[7]."

What does a company selling blinds have to do with your unique circumstances? Well, for starters, there is something we can learn from companies like Blinds to Go on how they achieve a growth-first culture. We'll discuss this in the next chapter.

Sales Multiplier Mindset: The purpose of an initial sale is to solidify additional selling opportunities that far exceed the value of the initial sale.

NOTES

1 https://www.demandgenreport.com/resources/research/2022-b2b-buyer-behavior-survey-orgs-must-remain-agile-as-buyers-conduct-self-service-anonymous-journeys/
2 https://en.wikipedia.org/wiki/Pontiac_Vibe
3 Many companies that develop new products continuously call themselves "innovative." These companies must be more aligned between product development, marketing, and sales. This disconnect often results in new products that don't sell or don't sell well. When this happens, product development blames marketing for ineffective campaigns; marketing blames sales for not introducing the product to customers.
4 https://en.wikipedia.org/wiki/Henry_Ford
5 https://www.investopedia.com/articles/personal-finance/061915/story-behind-teslas-success.asp
6 https://www2.deloitte.com/content/dam/Deloitte/ch/Documents/consumer-business/ch-en-consumer-business-made-to-order-consumer-review.pdf
7 https://www.blindstogo.com/en/about-us/careers/culture

2

Your Secret Ingredient to Multiply Sales

CUSTOMER NEEDS OVER COMPANY NEEDS

In Grade 3, I had a teacher named Ms. Taylor. She was known in our school to be very strict and didn't tolerate any of her students stepping out of line. My experience of her classroom was memorable, however, not for the reasons you might think. Ms. Taylor had little patience for any student she believed wasn't listening or paying attention. I recall being placed in the corner (facing the corner) on one occasion, being sent to the principal's office at least once for disrupting the classroom, and my parents receiving several notes throughout the year advising of my unacceptable behavior.

Ms. Taylor was very strict and was only sometimes pleased with my behavior. Interestingly, however, her perspective of my behavior was very different from that of Mr. Casey, my Grade 4 teacher. Mr. Casey was well liked by students and known for his sense of humor. If you were to walk by his classroom, you would most likely see him sitting on the edge of a desk, speaking one-on-one with students, and providing encouragement. Mr. Casey was far less strict than Ms. Taylor, so I had a far better experience. As a bonus, Mr. Casey didn't send home notes about my behavior and never sent me to the principal's office.

Recognizing that these teachers were teaching me during different years and that I was (presumably) maturing with age, you might think that Ms. Taylor's and Mr. Casey's experiences were potentially both accurate (which is what my parents believed to be the case). From my perspective, however, there was something else at play.

Today, my two boys are in school, and each has a different teacher every year. Similar to my experience, some teachers boast about the joys each of the boys have in their classroom, and others voice concerns over their behavior. As an example, a teacher of my youngest son recently sent us a

DOI: 10.4324/9781003463962-3

note home telling us what an excellent student he was. Unfortunately, this teacher moved schools mid-year, and she was replaced by a new teacher who, after a couple of months of teaching our son, sent an email to my wife suggesting he had difficulty paying attention in class.

How is it possible that these teachers, with similar education, working in the same schools and with the same students, have a very different experience? The answer is what I refer to as the personality bias. If you've ever completed a personality assessment such as Myers Briggs[1] or DiSC,[2] you'll know that one person may have multiple different thought patterns and behaviors. These differences are what make us unique. However, they also influence how we view and experience the world around us and the people within it.

One crucial observation emerges after incorporating these assessments in my work with sales teams for over a decade. Assessments help us recognize how we are different from everyone around us. Moreover, remembering we're all different helps us understand that every prospect, client, or customer is unique and different from us and other prospects, clients, or customers. You've heard the adage that what you say isn't as important as how you say it. This is true, but we need to dive deeper to understand how this applies to selling.

After facilitating these assessments with sales leaders and sales teams for over a decade, one of the most significant outcomes I've found from any behavioral assessment is recognizing ways to improve influence. Selling requires influence, which results from three fundamental skills: listening, observation, and positioning. When practiced correctly, it's these three core skills that allow us the best opportunity to apply influence, namely:

- Listening allows us to hear what our prospect or customer is requesting of us.
- Observation lets us see how we might position our response for the most significant impact.
- Language informs how we say what we say.

Suppose, for example, my goal is to understand your needs and, in turn, use this information to help me position my product or service in a way that you find appealing. In that case, I need to apply these three skills to sell you my solution (i.e., product or service).

Increasing one's influence to support selling is easy for sales professionals to grasp because, for the most part, their ability to sell and, in turn, maintain their job relies heavily on their ability to influence a customer to buy. The problem, however, is that sales are often only some of the roles in your company that interact with your prospects, customers, or clients.

Often, once a customer decides to make a purchase, they are introduced to others within the company, including (but not limited to) estimating, inside sales, customer service, operations, accounting, and others. These introductions may occur early in the sales process or immediately after a sale. Unless they've worked in sales, these other departments are at a disadvantage because they have not had the same exposure to the customer up to this point. Moreover, as a result, they need to recognize how their ability to listen, observe, and speak can directly influence a customer's desire to buy or buy again.

This might seem like a minor deal, as sales will often bring others involved with the customer up to speed on discussions, but unfortunately, that's where the communication stops. Rarely have I found any sales professionals continuing to keep these other departments informed on their ongoing observations, on what they've heard, and how they've positioned the sale (and its benefits and value) with the prospect. As you might imagine, this can create problems in the relationship with a customer. Hold on, though; it gets worse.

Not only are the departments outside of sales not trained in being influential, but they also have no incentive to be influential. You see, most departments outside of sales have their effectiveness measured in an entirely different way – it's based on their ability to be efficient and accurate. Let me clarify this statement with some examples.

Customer service is expected to address customer inquiries, concerns, or questions quickly and accurately. It is measured by how many customers it can manage and how quickly it can address those customers' needs.

Operations are expected to provide a service or a product that aligns with the companies' specifications as efficiently and cost-effectively as possible. Success is measured by how efficiently and accurately they can manage customer orders.

Accounts Receivable are measured based on their ability to manage customers or clients who have not yet paid, collect outstanding amounts, and minimize the list of slow-to-pay or non-paying accounts.

In other words, departments outside of sales have different expectations placed on them, and they are rewarded for focusing on company needs

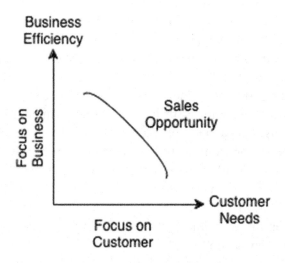

FIGURE 2.1

Denotes the Company over Customer Paradigm (Double-axis chart – listening on the left, efficiency on the bottom. As efficiency increases, listening goes down)

first and customer needs second. I call this the Company over Customer Paradigm (Figure 2.1).

To address the Company over Customer Paradigm, every department must be measured and rewarded for satisfying customer needs, which is the most critical performance measure. All departments and all employees must understand how their work influences the customer or client, both directly and indirectly. Moreover, the measures of their success in the role must be tied back to their ability to apply this influence.

This might sound like a lot of work, and it is. But for good reason.

WINNING THE RACE TO CAPTURE NEW CUSTOMERS

As I discussed in my book *The Unstoppable Sales Machine: How to Connect, Convert, and Close New Customers*, gathering customer intelligence is a crucial component of your sales process. At a macro level, understanding buyer demographics and how products or services are applied can provide insights into building an agile sales strategy to drive more sales. At a micro level, understanding buyer language around needs, objectives, and outcomes will support the development of targeted (and practical) messaging, language, and positioning, which all support closing more sales and increasing conversion rates.

This is more challenging than just capturing customer information, as there are gaps to consider that will impact your ability to gather meaningful customer intelligence.

Gap #1: Lack of Interaction with End-Users

If you leave the responsibility to your sales team to collect and share the customer intelligence they learn, then the information collected will be limited. In most instances, sales aren't in direct and ongoing contact with your customers' end-users, and therefore, you miss out on your customers' day-to-day feedback, resulting in a lack of information that can inform ongoing selling opportunities.

Gap #2: Failure to Accept Feedback from Sales

In my experience working with sales teams globally, other departments often dismiss the information and intelligence sales collect as either false or unusable. Suppose a customer complains about a product or service after buying it, and it even makes its way to sales. In that case, the departments involved often dismiss it as an unreasonable expectation of the customer or an unfulfillable promise made by sales during the sales process.

Gap #3: Employee Turnover in Customer Accounts

The employees who work within your existing customer's companies can change, which can affect your ability to continue selling to a customer. A study by Altrata suggested that turnover for C Suite positions in Fortune 1000 companies ranged from 11.8% for CEOs, all the way up to 27.3% for COOs.[3] Considering most buy decisions are escalated to the approval of someone in the C Suite, there is no guarantee your current customers will buy from you again.

Let's look at an example of why gathering customer intelligence is an organizational effort, not a sales effort.

Suppose a key decision-maker was to leave their role. Your sales team may gain insight into decision-makers leaving or being replaced if your customers share this information with them directly; however, rumors of key decision-maker departures often emerge at your customers internally, far before any career changes are posted on LinkedIn. As a result, sales are often the last to learn of the departures of key employees or decision-makers. Those most likely to learn first are your employees who interact with your customers daily, aka Customer Service, Inside Sales, Accounting, Operations, and so on.

The reality, then, is that collecting relevant, useful, and timely customer intelligence requires the efforts of both your sales team and your employees who interact with customers.

Learning of key employee departures is only one example of customer intelligence you could and should be collecting. Here is a list of the various other forms of customer intelligence that can enable you to increase your sales:

- Feedback on the fit, form, and function of your product or service.
- Ideas to improve your product or service.
- Suggestions for changes in your customer or client support processes.
- Feedback from testing of new products or services.
- Opportunities to improve the quality of your product, service, or delivery methods.
- Insights into new products or services to support your customer.
- New partnership opportunities with existing customers or client suppliers or vendors.
- Feedback on the performance of partners who support your product or service.
- Recommendations to improve processes or methods to enhance customer experience.
- Referral opportunities to other potential customers or clients.[4]

It's easy to see the positive impact that timely and accurate customer intelligence can have on your future sales, so the real question becomes, who should capture information, and to what degree? The answer to this question is most often determined by the size and structure of your company; however, here are some examples to choose from.

1. Position or Title
2. Information Collected
3. Benefit to the Company

Example #1:

Customer Service or Customer Support
Improvement to existing products or services
Insights on enhancements to existing offerings

Example #2:

> Production or Operations
> Improvements to product or service delivery quality
> Development of new products/services

Example #3:

> Accounts Receivable
> Customers with financial difficulties
> Shifts in pricing or payment terms, and economic slowdowns

Example #4:

> Reception
> Customer inquiries and availability of departmental contacts
> Changes to staff availability and the need to increase customer responsiveness

Example #5:

> Shipping and receiving
> Customer slowdowns or shutdowns, and key competitors
> Insights into customer demand changes, and competitors

Example #6:

> Engineering
> Product or service design flaws or necessary changes
> Confirmation of desirable changes to products or services

Example #7:

> Technical Support
> Frequency and severity of customer technical issues
> Prioritization of product, service, or support changes

If everyone who interacts with your customers directly and indirectly solicits information, you'll likely face a new challenge. How can you collect customer intelligence in a meaningful, actionable way?

CUSTOMER INTELLIGENCE TO MULTIPLY SALES

When I was 14, I landed a job at a local grocery store, A&P (Atlantic and Pacific Company). Initially, my role consisted of three tasks:

- Packing groceries at the customer check-out.
- Collecting and corralling shopping carts for customers to take upon entry to the store.
- Sweeping and mopping areas around the entry and exit doors.

My exposure to these seemingly simple tasks gave me insights that even the store managers and supervisors didn't have.

One such example was in how to fill the cart corral area. I learned that filling the cart corral area made it more difficult for customers to enter the store during peak busy periods (the carts were just inside the door). The carts were only eight feet from the entry door when the corral was full. Inside the entry door was a stand containing the weekly shopping flyer, and most often, customers who took a cart would stop to pick up and read the flyer. As a result, there would usually be a minor traffic jam of customers standing in front of the cart corral, thereby blocking new customers trying to enter the store and grab a cart (or a flyer).

If I filled the cart corral to 75% of its capacity, it left enough room for new customers to enter the store and move around the customers standing and reviewing the flyer. It didn't result in any customers being stuck standing in the entryway. My realization came one day after an older man complained to me about having to wait in line to get his cart. "Why don't you just put fewer carts in the coral, so people aren't lined up out the door?" he asked.

The gentleman's question made logical sense and forced me to rethink how I perceived somebody should handle the cart-filling operation. What would happen when, after being called to the front of the store to fill the cart corral, I only filled it to 75% of its capacity? Based on catching the Assistant Store Manager rolling his eyes when he noticed me walking away from the jammed cart area, I was lazy.

One day, Alex, a co-worker, asked me why I had only partially filled the cart corral. He suggested I fill the corral to 100% or more of its capacity, allowing me more time to step away from monitoring carts and focus on other tasks. I explained my reasoning, and after glancing at the carts, Alex responded, "You're likely right, but I hate filling carts." With that, he walked away and continued jamming the corral full of carts and delaying the entry of new customers to the store.

I share this example not to suggest that no one else observed the problems the cart corral created but that each employee had their own perception of the responsibilities of their role. My perception, influenced strongly by my customer interaction, was that my role was to keep carts filled but ensure new customers could quickly and easily enter the store. If that meant more frequent visits to the front of the store to check on the number of carts in the corral, so be it. Remember that we live in the north, so customers forced to wait in line for a cart might be forced to stand in the rain, sleet, snow, or ice-cold wind while waiting to enter the store.

When you consider all the customer intelligence your employees gather daily, and often inadvertently, the mere thought of attempting to capture the information can become overwhelming. In my example above, suppose that the store management had asked me why I was only filling carts to 75% capacity, let's also assume they thought my reasoning was sound; what would they need to do to adopt this change for all stock clerks moving forward? Likely, they would have placed a letter or policy change in the employee cafeteria to communicate the new cart policy. If they wanted to take this one step further, they would have asked store supervisors to review this policy with their teams.

But this is just a straightforward example. What would happen if the store manager listened to all the ideas for improvement that customers and employees were sharing? Most likely, they'd be overwhelmed with information, needing help prioritizing what changes or enhancements get acted upon and when. This is one of the most significant objections I receive when discussing the importance of collecting customer intelligence today. There's too much information to collect, organize, and do something with.

Fortunately, there are simple ways to collect customer intelligence, from simple surveys to customer suggestion boxes to notes captured from customer discussions. The most crucial consideration when collecting this information is how you want to access the information and the format in which you'd prefer to share it.

Here are some examples of different methods to collect customer intelligence you can implement. Below I'll define each as follows:

1. Collection method selected
2. Where information is located
3. How the information is used and pros or cons for each.

Using Customer Relationship Management (CRM) software

1. Placed in a field easily accessible under a "Company Record."
2. Information is accessible for reports.
3. Data is quickly reviewed for trends and emerging issues. It is reliant on employees to enter information.

Using Shared Documents (i.e., Google Drive)

1. Placed in a shared folder that is easily accessible by all parties.
2. Information can be sorted and reviewed for follow-up and action.
3. Data can be easily accessed and modified as necessary. It is reliant on employees to enter information.

Using Internal Chat Software (i.e., Teams, Slack)

1. Shared with pre-determined groups, departments, or individuals for response and action.
2. Information is shared for quick response by the appropriate department.
3. Employees can quickly drop information into the chat.
4. Unable to generate reports and information can be distracting.

Using External Chat Software (i.e., Tidio, LiveChat)

1. Most chat software allows for surveys and storing of customer responses.
2. Information can be shared in reports, often customizable depending on the software.
3. Ease of access and viewing of data. Most customers leave a chat before responding to a survey.

Using Automated Survey Tools[5]

1. Most electronic tools offer cloud-based storage of customer responses.
2. Reports can be easily generated, allowing for analysis of trends or gaps.
3. Ease of reporting: A de-personalized means of collecting information, resulting in reduced value.

Collecting customer intelligence is fundamental to informing how you sell what you sell (and how to sell more of it!) and *foundational to your sales multiplier formula*. Your goal isn't to solicit information to improve your product or service but to gather intelligence that allows you to sell more of it to existing and new customers.

How can we convert all this information into more sales without burying ourselves in data and information in the process? Let me tell you how.

TURNING INTELLIGENCE INTO USEFUL OUTCOMES

By this point, you've likely realized some additional opportunities to collect information from your customer or client interactions that can be useful. There likely remain three questions to be answered:

1. How should you capture this information?
2. How can you convert information to actionable outcomes?
3. How will these outcomes directly result in generating more sales?

The information you collect can quickly become overwhelming and take on the form of "Big Data." The problem with big data is exactly that, it's most often "too big" for it to be useful. The key, then, is if you are going to collect information from customers at various points in their journey, it's got to be useful, but not for the reason you might suspect.

Most customer experience experts will advise that collecting customer information provides you the intelligence to "stand out" and become a "leader" in your industry or sector. It would be great if you could cash this hard-earned status to the bank. Most often, you can't.

My view, and the one that I assist clients with introducing, is that investing the time and effort into gathering, deciphering, and applying intelligence collected through customer interactions is only a valuable investment IF it results in net new sales. By this, I am referring to an increase in the value of an existing order, the generation of new orders, the generation of new opportunities, and/or the opening of new accounts. Seem impossible? Let me give you an example.

We own an R.V. trailer, which we've used for camping since our boys were younger. If you've ever owned an R.V., you'll know that they require maintenance, particularly if you need to store them for any period. Living in the northern hemisphere, we typically get snow each winter, and therefore, we must "winterize" our R.V., remove the battery, add antifreeze to the water lines, and perform a few other small tasks. All this happens before we store the trailer for about six months.

Each year, our list of winterization tasks gets a bit longer because of the problems we encounter. For example, I typically drain all the water and add antifreeze in early November. However, a few years ago, snow came in late October before I had the chance to winterize the R.V., resulting in frozen lines and a cracked faucet (you'd be surprised at the damage ice can do in water lines). Now, I begin my winterization earlier each year.

One of the more critical winterization activities we practice is to place bars of soap and dryer sheets throughout the R.V., as this is supposed to ward off any rodents. I don't know if it does; fortunately, any signs of rodents have been minimal. I recently went to our local R.V. repair shop to pick up some antifreeze in preparation for winterizing our R.V. I noticed a new product designed to ensure rodents don't come near your trailer. They were in the form of small packets, and after reading the label, I decided to try them.

The young lady who was ringing up my order politely asked the size of my trailer. Confused, I responded and then asked why this was important. She replied that the rodent repellant was to be placed a certain distance apart to be effective, so the longer the trailer, the more product I would need to buy.

When I shared that our trailer was 23′ long, she responded that I should add another box of the product if I wanted it to be effective. That's where the conversation took a turn. As I reached for another box of the repellant, she pointed to a printed flyer on the counter and said, "We can also apply it for you in liquid form, spraying it on the undercarriage of the trailer." Curious, I asked what the benefit of this application was. "For starters, we spray it on the outside, which ensures rodents never enter your trailer. Our application also includes a guarantee."

For someone who has committed their career to sales, it was apparent what was happening; she was attempting to upsell me, using intelligence gained from our discussion. You might be thinking, "But Shawn, she is working the counter in retail, so that's her job," but it's quite the contrary. This was different from the usual person I dealt with at the counter when I visited the store, so curious, I asked her what her role was. "Well, my official job is bookkeeper, but I help where possible."

Here is someone who isn't in a customer-facing role but happens to be interacting with a customer. By asking a couple of simple questions and with the intention of helping the customer, they upsold me on what I intended to buy.

When I bought the more expensive application package, I told the young lady, "You should be in sales!" to which she quickly responded, "No thanks, no offense, but I have no desire to interact with customers on a regular basis." This response wasn't surprising to me, and if you follow the steps I lay out in this book, you should be prepared to hear a similar statement from your employees. In upcoming chapters, we'll talk more about overcoming this objection that many of your non-customer-facing employees will have.

Considering this example and our discussions thus far, consider the following:

1. You have dozens, possibly hundreds of employees (not in sales) who interact directly and indirectly with your customers daily.
2. These employees gain valuable insights into your customers' preferences, needs, demands, and expectations.
3. These insights can provide you with the intelligence and foresight to improve your products or services, identify new products or services, and further differentiate from your competition.
4. You can use this intelligence and gain further intel if you strategically collect this information in ways that can be reviewed, deciphered, and analyzed.
5. Using this information enables you to generate new selling opportunities, such as upsells, resells, referrals, and more.

In the next chapter, we'll discuss how you can use this intelligence to generate more sales with less effort (and without hiring more salespeople). If this sounds like something you'd be interested in (and I'm wondering why you wouldn't be), then let's jump to the next chapter!

Sales Multiplier Mindset: All departments and all employees must understand how their work influences the customer or client, both directly and indirectly.

NOTES

1 https://en.wikipedia.org/wiki/Myers%E2%80%93Briggs_Type_Indicator
2 https://en.wikipedia.org/wiki/DISC_assessment
3 https://altrata.com/reports/c-suite-turnover-2023
4 Author's Note: We'll discuss referral opportunities in future chapters.
5 Automated surveys are my least favorite method of requesting customer information as they are de-personalized and don't allow for more in-depth questions to clarify concerns raised. Those who answer surveys are either extremely happy with their experience or extremely dissatisfied, which often represents about 20% of your customers, meaning 80% don't participate.

3

Selling Isn't Just for Sales

We need to recognize that the initial sale is a gateway to multiplying your sales (read that twice). Once your customers or clients have been exposed to your company and purchased your products or services, it is other employees, those who typically don't reside in the sales department, whom they will build relationships with. Some examples of these employees can include engineering, administration, production, and customer service.

As a result, employees outside the sales department are often a much-needed resource who determine (and have more significant influence over) whether a customer buys more, or ever buys again. Suppose, for example, a customer's experience with the rest of your employees is positive. In that case, they will be eager to learn more ways to work with your company and possibly even refer others. However, if their experience is not so positive (despite a great experience with sales), chances are any future sales or referrals won't happen. Additionally, what are the chances that when a customer is considering an upsell, cross-sell, or referring your company to a possible new customer, sales are immediately available and ready to jump in? It's doubtful (and if your sales team is waiting and immediately available for customers to discuss these new opportunities, how much time are they spending prospecting?).

FINDING TIME TO DEVELOP NEW SELLING OPPORTUNITIES

As a result of the above, multiplying your sales requires that we shift our perspective around who interacts with customers or clients and what those interactions can consist of. A recent study published by Gartner[1]

DOI: 10.4324/9781003463962-4

suggested that most sales today are made by what Gartner calls "Buying Teams." The teams Gartner refers to consist of those who work in a wide variety of roles at your customer's company and who have influence over the buying decision (although they may not have the final decision). Think about each customer you have today, including decision-makers and decision-influencers. The former has the final say over who the company buys from. However, the latter (decision-influencers) have an increasing influence over the decision-maker and the final decision they make. How might this play out for your company today?

Suppose you were to make a sale to a customer. Leading up to the sale, it was sales who met with the decision-maker (the person who makes the "buy" decision), as well as several other people, the "decision-influencers" (this may have included various departments with questions, perspectives, needs, etc.). Making the final sale and influencing the decision-maker came down to addressing the concerns of these different departments and those of the decision-makers themselves. In other words, there were several people with whom an interaction occurred (and was necessary) to bring the sale to a close.

Here are some examples of the various meetings and interactions that may take place today for your company to close a sale:

- A meeting with Engineering (decision-influencer), who is seeking your product or solution, and once satisfied, makes an introduction to Purchasing[2] (decision-influencer), who, after reviewing multiple quotes, issues the PO on behalf of their organization.
- A meeting with a company Vice President or Executive (decision-maker) who then makes an introduction to others within the company (decision-influencers) before they collectively agree to purchase your service or product.
- A meeting with Human Resources (decision-influencer), who connects you with Operations and Finance (also decision-influencers), following which they introduce you to the President (decision-maker) who decides to invest in your product or services.

Notice that sometimes you may meet with a decision-maker who introduces you to decision-influencers, seeking their input, perspectives, and support in making the final "buy" decision. In other situations, you may gain entry to the company via a decision-influencer. Whatever the sequence of interactions that leads to closing the sale, in virtually every sale made today, multiple people are involved.

The key, then for sales professionals, is to cast a broad net, focusing on seeking out and pursuing decision-makers and the pursuit of trusted relationships with decision-influencers. Although this is possible (and the approach I recommend in my *Unstoppable Sales Prospecting Program*), the reality is sales aren't always in the best position to or knowledgeable enough to address the vast array of questions that may be asked of them by all these different roles. For example, I've worked with:

1. Medical equipment sales professionals who are asked and respond to a wide variety of questions from Nursing staff, Hospital Engineers, Doctors, and the hospital's Chief Medical Officer.
2. Capital equipment sales professionals in the mining industry who field questions from Mine Managers, Maintenance Managers, Maintenance Technicians, General Managers, and Mining staff.
3. Commercial insurance agents who respond to questions shared by Business Owners, Company Executives, Human Resources, Finance, and others.

When you consider the wide variety of people and roles involved in influencing or making the buying decision, is it reasonable to believe that sales have the necessary information, expertise, and knowledge to answer the vast array of questions they will receive? The short answer is "not likely." But let's take this one step further.

You might expect sales to bridge internal connections between the company's subject matter experts and those with the expertise and information to address prospect or customer inquiries and then share this with the prospect or customers. Okay, but how much time does it take to share this information, monitor responses, book meetings, and manage this flow of information? Let me help you; it takes a lot of time! This time is better spent searching for the next sales opportunity. Despite the best of intentions, you and I both know that in this chain of broken communication, something will eventually fall through the cracks.

When sales have the full support of others within the company, assisting them in building and nurturing prospect and customer relationships and responding to prospect or customer questions, suddenly selling, be it new sales, upsells or cross-sells, and the influence required to generate these sales become significantly easier and more predictable, and they tend to multiply much faster.

To put it bluntly, then, if you want to multiply your sales, you are going to need to get others in your organization involved, not just because of their expertise and the desire to ensure your prospects or customers have rapid and accurate responses to their inquiries and needs, but because the Sales Time Paradox will otherwise hold you back.

THE SALES TIME PARADOX

If you were to make a sale today, you'd have invested time in various activities to do so. Some of these activities directly result in sales, such as meeting or calling a prospect and converting them to a paying customer. You'll also have spent time on other indirect activities, including researching new prospects, preparing for sales meetings, traveling, following up with existing prospects, participating in internal sales meetings, and so on.

When new employees begin working in sales, they invest significant time learning about and understanding the products or services, the sales processes, and even getting to know other members of the sales team and key employees within the company. As time progresses, less time is spent in this "learning" mode, and attention turns to spending time on direct and indirect activities to generate sales. Unfortunately, for most employees new to sales, the time available for "direct selling activities" often peaks around six months. After this, indirect selling activities absorb more time, leading to lower productivity and sales effectiveness. Figure 3.1 demonstrates this shift in how time is devoted to selling and the impact on sales outcomes.

Why does time that is devoted to direct selling decline? There can be a wide variety of reasons. However, four of the most common include:

1. Customers (who get to know the salesperson through their initial interactions) continue to contact them after becoming a customer with additional questions, concerns, or inquiries unrelated to making extra sales.
2. Other departments begin involving the salesperson in issues related to their customers, which can include customer complaints, order

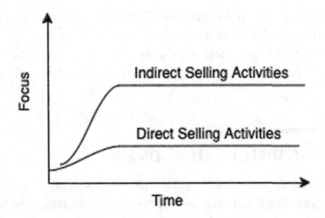

FIGURE 3.1

Direct selling peaks, replaced by increasing indirect selling time

changes, design changes, payment issues, and so on. This often involves emails (requesting a response) and meetings.

3. Internal departments engage sales in meetings related to changes in internal processes that can impact their customers (or customers in general) to gain their perspective or feedback on customer-related issues, process changes, and so on. This might include discussions related to quality or delivery issues.

4. Salespeople are often expected to participate in new product or service design and implementation, which can take the form of meetings, team calls, or emails. In addition, requests to trial and/or gain feedback from customers on new products or services are also quite common.

You'll notice that I didn't reference a loss of motivation or a decline in the desire to sell, but let's be honest: new sales professionals are typically eager to make their first sales. However, this eagerness can diminish over time, partially on account of their having "proven themselves" by creating a sale and partially because as they become known internally, they start getting pulled into a wide variety of meetings, emails, and discussions that have little to do with making a sale.

This erosion of direct selling time happens ever so slowly. The salesperson then, who is asked to invest their time in an increasing number of indirect selling activities, often assumes this is a natural evolution of their role and, therefore, isn't concerned about less time being available for direct selling.

I call this phenomenon the *Sales Time Paradox*; in my experience, it is the number one contributor to diminishing sales in companies today. The question then isn't to what degree the sales time paradox impacts your ability to sell, but how do you avoid it from impacting your direct selling time?

INCREASING DIRECT SELLING TIME

You might have experienced the sales time paradox, with your sales often taking the form of a flat or even a decline over time. You might be busy as a sales professional but don't have the sales to show for it. A natural response to flat or declining sales is to dive into sales training or new selling tools or software, with increasing pressure mounting from sales leadership (or the sales team) to start generating more (new) sales.

Faced with declining sales and this pressure, sales leaders (who are already under pressure to meet ever-increasing sales targets annually) place undue pressure on sales to generate more opportunities, which in turn leads to burnout, dissension among sales, and, in some instances, key sales professionals leaving the company. The solution then shifts from training to a need to hire more people (often a last resort). We're throwing more money at a problem with nothing to do with skills or hiring. Is this vaguely familiar?

But wait, it can (and likely will) get much worse.

Many sales leaders, faced with flat or declining sales, begin to hold more meetings with their sales teams to "help" them sell more. They add more one-to-one meetings to dive into each salesperson's activities, "coaching them" to help them to be more successful. Although this can assist some team members with closing complex or challenging prospects, the time spent together also creates more … you guessed it, indirect selling time. Which in turn means there is less time available for direct selling activities. Do you see an alarming trend here?

Outside of the impact an increase in indirect selling activities can have on generating new sales if you expect your sales team to manage existing customer accounts, this spiral can get much worse. Let me explain.

Depending on what you sell, it's not uncommon to expect the sales to "manage" the accounts they close. There may be an expectation that sales periodically check in with their customer accounts to ensure things are running smoothly, follow up on any outstanding customer issues, and generally do what is necessary to keep customers happy. This type of "account management" activity is often given to sales as they are the ones "with the customer relationship."

Logically, this might make sense; however, as you've seen, all these activities are indirect, with some even falling on the side of administrative. Aside from the decline in the time available for the salesperson to sell, leaving the customer or client relationship solely in the hands of sales can lead to other problems, for example:

> Isolating relationships to sales only creates a reliance on each person in sales to sustain customer relationships. If someone leaves the company, the customer relationship is at risk.
>
> Assigning administrative tasks to sales (such as invoice collection) reduces the time to find and close *new* accounts.
>
> Placing sales in the position of taking the lead on customer issues (i.e., overdue invoices, customer complaints, concerns with quality) shifts the dynamic of the customer relationship, which, in some instances, makes it difficult for them to sustain a positive relationship with the customer, further hindering opportunities to upsell, resell, or cross-sell.
>
> When you move customer relationship management entirely to sales, you send a message to the rest of your employees – *don't worry about the customer; that's the salesperson's job.*

The real question you need to consider is to what extent *sales should be involved in* managing customers and their accounts.

If sales are to focus solely on selling, then I recommend moving account management activities to another role. Alternatively, if your sales team makes more sense to manage the accounts they close *and* you expect them to find, convert, and close new accounts, then you must monitor and manage time closely. In this situation, no more than 30% of the time is spent managing existing accounts (even if there is an opportunity to sell these new accounts). You are leaving 20% of the time available to address "Account Administrative" issues and the remaining 50% to pursue new sales opportunities (which involves research, outreach, initial meetings, writing proposals, etc.).

To accomplish this and minimize the impact of the Sales Time Paradox, map out how your selling time is spent because it's common for account management activities to slowly increase over time as customers, employees, and sales do their utmost to ensure customers are retained. Think of this like maintaining your car. As the car ages, you need to spend more time (and more money) keeping it to ensure it doesn't break down or leave you stranded. Your customers or clients require more maintenance over time if you want to maintain their accounts.

When you consider that most people who enter the sales profession do so with the desire to have more freedom in how they spend their time, monitoring and managing their time can be perceived as micro-managing, which can lead to employee retention issues.

Confused? I understand. Fortunately, however, there is a better way.

MANAGING ACCOUNTS IS NOT SELLING

Many of my friends, and my wife's friends, are people we've known for 20 years or more. Several years ago, I met a friend, Don, who was introduced to me by someone I've known since high school. We met while I was out of town on a motorcycle ride, and over time, we became close friends. When Don first came to our home, I introduced him to my wife and our two boys. While traveling across Canada and the United States on various motorcycle trips, I introduced Don to any of my friends we encountered.

Although I don't see Don as often as I used to due to our work and travel schedules, we remain in contact, and my boys still ask, "How is Don?"

I share this to demonstrate that the relationship I developed with Don remains strong today because I didn't isolate Don from my relationships or network; I invited him in. We create stronger relationships with others when we expose them to the relationships we have with others. Similarly, we shouldn't isolate our customer relationships to our sales department.

There are three reasons why your customer relationships should be owned by the entire organization, not just the sales department.

To begin with, sales don't own the customer relationship; they develop it. So, having sales handle everything from following up on invoices to communicating delays with shipping or service delivery is the wrong approach if your goals are to ensure sales continue focusing their time on selling and bringing on new customers. You avoid the Sales Time Suck from occurring and eroding time available to sell.

Second, when we set the expectation that our customer relationships are the sole responsibility of our sales team, or we set the expectation that they own the relationship, we isolate the rest of our team (i.e., finance, operations, engineering, administration, production, technical support) from the customer. These various other departments' decisions are made in consideration of what the customer needs or wants rather than what would be best for the company (or the department). In these situations, the customer is often an afterthought due to the need to understand who the customer is, what they seek from our company, and how we can ensure we remain relevant and helpful to them in the future.

Here are some common examples of how a customer relationship isolated to the sales department can impact your company. Take a minute to determine which of these might exist within your organization:

- Operations change internal processes to increase efficiency, which can negatively impact customers.
- Finance identifies and introduces payment terms that are ideal for your company without validating if they are acceptable (and reasonable) to your customers.
- Engineering design is a new product or service that does not meet your customer's needs, resulting in either a lack of sales or additional design work, thereby delaying introduction to the market and increasing the overall cost of design.
- Technical support provides a ticketing system designed to capture how they spend time (down to the minute), encouraging quick resolution to customer issues or concerns but also encouraging rapid closure of tickets without ensuring the solution has fully satisfied the need of the customer (which leads to them logging another ticket).

The goal *should be* to create a sense of ownership for your customer among everyone in the company. When everyone in the company clearly understands your customers, including their specific needs and demands, employees shift their focus from "getting work done" to "doing the work that best supports customer needs." That's the ingredients to happy customers, who are retained and buy more.

Recognizing you might fear that this kind of shift distracts employees from being productive, it's quite the contrary. Efficiency is the foundation for customer satisfaction. Doing work efficiently (and effectively) that supports the customer provides them with the rapid response and resolute they seek.

Viewing the customer relationship as something everyone on the team needs to become aware of, familiar with, and involved in shifts employees away from focusing on their own priorities to the priorities of customers or clients. Here are some examples of why a broader ownership of the customer relationship is beneficial:

> Engineering needs close customer relationships with whom it can engage while designing or improving a product or service.
> Operations should connect with the customer and feel confident in discussing process changes to ensure they have no negative impact on the customer.
> Finance should view customer relationships as partners with whom they will work closely to ensure that payment schedules benefit both the customer and the company.

When you leave the customer relationship solely in the hands of sales, the remainder of employees are left in a bubble. This means the focus turns solely to what is best for the company without considering whether it is also good for the customer. Unless you have (and expect to continue to have) a monopoly in what you sell, this is a recipe for disaster and the fastest way to ensure customers begin considering your competitors' offers.

Aside from the obvious benefits you can gain from building stronger connections between your employees and the customer, you also make a foundation to multiply your sales.

Wait, what?

That's right. Even if the Sales Time Paradox directly influences sales, you can still multiply your sales without completely changing how salespeople spend their time. In fact, by taking the steps we'll discuss next and engaging your broader team in your customer or client relationships, you can introduce methods that will multiply your sales without hiring more salespeople and without attempting to micromanage how your sales team spends their time.

OBSESS OVER THESE (OR YOU'LL LOSE SALES)

Before I introduce the "Sales Multiplier" framework to demonstrate how you can generate more sales, let's highlight a few of the priorities you'll need to set to ensure the framework has the intended impact on your sales.

Let me start by saying that these priorities are things you'll need to obsess over. The reason I chose the word "obsess" is that it highlights the amount of effort, focus, and consistency you'll need to have if you are to ensure your entire organization embraces the sales multiplier framework as a way of doing business. To obsess is to preoccupy or fill the mind of someone continually and intrusively. Although this word may carry some negative connotations, think of "obsessing" as constantly sharing the same messages, priorities, and desired outcomes for each of these priorities despite the feedback or pushback you receive.

Priorities to Obsess Over While Introducing Your Sales Multiplier Framework:

1. Obsess over the journey of each new customer or client.
2. Obsess over building customer connections for each role within the company.
3. Obsess over collecting and learning from customer feedback and input.
4. Obsess over maximizing the revenue potential of each customer.
5. Obsess over following the Sales Multiplier framework.

Obsess over the Journey of Each New Customer

When I mention customer journey, your mind likely jumps to considering the different steps or stages each new customer transitions through once they become a customer. These stages may include awareness of your product or service, interaction with sales, customer onboarding, product or service delivery, and customer retention – all very common stages of the customer journey.

The Sales Multiplier framework, however, requires that you consider the customer journey from a different perspective, identifying the selling opportunity for each customer as they progress through their journey with your company. Figure 3.2 identifies these stages.

Most people think about the customer journey differently, which is precisely why retaining customers and selling more to existing customers can be challenging for many companies. Your "obsession" over this new way of looking at the journey is necessary as you need to reorient how everyone in the company thinks about this journey. We don't sell to a customer to build a relationship with them; we sell to create a relationship that results in ongoing selling opportunities!

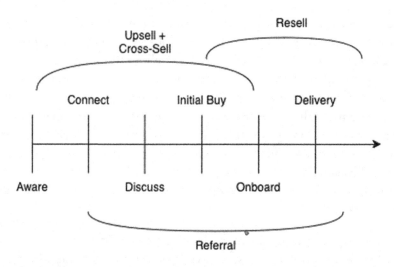

FIGURE 3.2

Stages in the customer journey, with upsell, cross-sell, resell, and referral added in

Obsess over Building Customer Connections for Each Role

Creating an expectation that all departments will connect with and support the customer relationship is not enough to ensure new selling opportunities. When you introduce a change such as this, most employees will struggle with:

1. Identifying how to integrate these connections into their existing work.
2. How to measure the impact of these connections (i.e., What's the benefit of doing this?).
3. Making this a priority given their various other priorities.

To ensure these connections become a priority, you must obsess over the importance of these connections and how they will support each department and the company. Some Examples of how you can develop these connections as a priority include:

Setting annual targets or goals for each department in building these connections.

Creating metrics for each department that encourage consistent customer interaction.

Sharing examples of the positive impacts of customer relationships in each department.

Frequent mentioning of the benefits and outcomes experienced through solid customer connections.

Using surveys to measure customer experience in working with different departments.

Obsess over Collecting and Learning from Customer Intelligence

When each department builds and sustains customer connections, it gains insights into how customers operate, their challenges and weaknesses, and, most importantly, opportunities to improve how it sells, serves, and supports its customers. In other words, it gains first-hand knowledge of exactly how to build a competitive advantage for its company, allowing it to differentiate itself in the market.

Insights from customer connections are better captured through one-to-one interactions with customers and surveys conducted by each department[3], and observations from various interactions with customers.

I call these insights customer intelligence because they provide you with the exact information needed to determine how to sell more of your products or services, what new products or services to sell, and what changes or improvements are necessary to increase the sales of what you already sell.

For each department, you must identify what customer intelligence they can gather and then obsess over its collection and application. What have they learned, and how are they applying it?

Obsess over Maximizing the Revenue Potential of Each Customer

Earlier, I mentioned how isolating your customer or client relationships to sales can also isolate the understanding and ownership of revenue generation to sales. In other words, limiting the relationship to sales can (and often will) result in a "us first, customer second" mentality for your team. Not only does this create problems for attempting to retain customers, but it also limits your ability to maximize the revenue potential of each customer.

For example, customer service, shipping, or operations are often in the best position to determine what new services, support, or products would improve the customer's experience. They gain insights into who the competition is, what gaps exist in how it supports the customer, and when and where opportunities to upsell, cross-sell, or resell the customer first arise. I'm not suggesting these departments should be the first to make these sales (although they can!). However, they are in the best position to assess when and what the selling opportunity is.

Obsess about helping each department recognize the revenue potential for your customers or clients, how they can identify new opportunities to sell, and what they should do when these opportunities arise.

Obsess over Following the Sales Multiplier Framework

You will need to drive the sales multiplier framework. It can't be passed off to the Vice President of Sales or someone leading sales, as they don't have the authority over other executives or leaders to reinforce (or enforce) its application.

If you obsess over the points listed above, then reinforcing the application of the sales multiplier framework becomes a way to tie these other focus areas together. Here are some examples:

- Obsessing over the journey of each new customer reinforces the need to understand every aspect of the customer interaction, which allows to position new selling opportunities when time and need present themselves.
- Obsessing over building customer connections for each role ensures that all roles recognize the impact and opportunity to support each customer to improve their experience and the value they receive from your company. Most importantly, this is the foundation of building a culture that puts sales ahead of support and realizes that sales are the primary reason you find and support customers in the first place.
- Obsessing about collecting and learning from customer intelligence builds an awareness of the importance of collecting and, most importantly, sharing information gained from interactions with customers. It supports data-driven decision-making relative to new products, new services, and additional sales opportunities rather than drawing upon assumptions or instincts about what customers want that aren't supported or true.

When you obsess over maximizing each customer's revenue potential, you reinforce the importance of sales and place it as the primary driver for the customer relationship. Too many employees believe their role is the most important in the company. Overcoming this bias is necessary to build a culture that serves and sells, helping all employees realize that without a sale (or sales), there would be no customer, no company, and no job for them to attend to.

Next, let's spend a few minutes discussing how customers buy in today's market and how insights from these buying behaviors will feed your sales multiplier framework to generate more sales.

Sales Multiplier Mindset: The question then isn't to what degree the sales time paradox impacts your ability to sell, but how do you avoid it from impacting your direct selling time?

NOTES

1 https://www.gartner.ca/en/sales/insights/b2b-buying-journey
2 Author's Note: Purchasing or Procurement are exceptional cases in that they are rarely decision-makers but have the authority to purchase according to specific criteria set by the decision-maker.
3 Note: I'm not a fan of electronic surveys, as they limit your ability to capture usable information. A Net Promoter Score, for example, doesn't tell me what I need to know to understand why the customer scored us as they did.

4

Selling Today Is a Team Sport

Think of the last time you made a relatively significant purchase. Be it a car, appliance, or a home. Although your primary interaction was likely with a salesperson, other factors influenced your buying decision. For example, if you purchased a new vehicle, you are likely to have either spoken with someone in service or asked friends or colleagues about the "reputation" of the service team at the dealership you were considering. If you purchased a home, you interacted with a realtor, lawyer, home inspector, and possibly new neighbors before deciding.

These are all examples of consumer sales. However, as mentioned in the previous chapter, studies such as Gartner's "New B2B Buying Journey and Its Implications"[1] have repeatedly demonstrated that even corporate buying is moving to a team-focused model, with more people involved in the buy decision and more time spent by these groups comparing, contrasting, and discussing their buy preferences.

To support and influence these teams requires more than just a salesperson. After all, you can't expect sales to be the experts in all areas of your product or service and expect them to act as the "go-between" between a customer buying team and your company is unrealistic. Your customers have many questions, and they expect answers almost immediately.

In other words, the historic "lone wolf" salesperson who, through some mystic powers, was able to repeatedly bring new customers to your door is gone. To sell today requires you to fight fire with fire; in this case, you meet team-based buying with team-based selling.

DOI: 10.4324/9781003463962-5

TEAM-BASED SELLING

On the surface, this might seem like a common-sense approach, and it is. The problem, however, is that common sense isn't always so common. As discussed previously, most often departments outside of sales view "sales" as someone else's job.

The barriers to fully embracing and adopting team-based selling and, in turn, capitalizing on this approach to generate new selling opportunities are often dismissed in favor of focusing on priorities more aligned with each department's fundamental role. I refer to this as the Sales-Centric Bias, and it exists in nearly every organization in which individuals within an organization have no experience working in sales and possess a lack of understanding of how to sell and, as a result, place sales as the responsibility of someone else, most often the sales department.

Let me be clear: The Sales-Centric Bias likely exists in your company today, and its mere existence means that the strategies we'll discuss (and you'll attempt to introduce) are likely to be met with resistance and plenty of it. Fortunately, you can take steps to mitigate and even overcome this bias.

OVERCOMING THE SALES-CENTRIC BIAS

Let's begin with what we know to be true. We are all, regardless of title, in sales. Although someone's role may differ in tasks or assignments from a customer-facing role, they still need to *sell* their ideas, needs, and opinions to others. Moreover, and as we discussed in earlier chapters, aside from using sales skills in this manner, every employee has a direct *and* indirect influence on your customers, which in turn influences their willingness and ability to buy more, buy again, and refer others (the secret behind the sales multiplier formula!). Heck, why do you think customer experience is such a hot topic? A positive customer experience aims to ensure your customers return to buy more and refer others. That's right, it's sales in disguise!

How can you get more people in your company aligned to support selling? If you are a sales leader, we'll dive deeper into this in Chapter 9. For now, let's focus on the simple steps you can take to build your team in support of selling.

Focus initially on shifting perspectives on sales. In other words, help those around you recognize that sales and the skills involved in selling are not something to be feared or despised but valuable skills that can help every employee be more effective in their role. When employees embrace this perspective (along with new skills and methods to complement their role in support of the customer), magical things happen.

Here are some specific examples participants in my Trusted Advisor program have shared with me because of our work together, helping them embrace sales and their role in helping to "sell and influence" customers:

Example #1: Reception realized customers who call to speak with someone don't want to be immediately "patched through to voice mail" when they call. Therefore, it would be valuable to offer them the option to call back when the employee is back in the office (which this receptionist had access to).

Example #2: Accounts Receivable, who historically sent templated and impersonal emails to customers about overdue accounts and demanding payments, have shared that being more personal and providing the customer options for payment, when possible, create a more positive experience for the customer and can influence them to invest in buying more products.

Example #3: Marketing teams have spent more time with sales in customer meetings, which has helped them to understand their customers better and, as a result, have been able to develop more influential messaging and offers that attract more ideal customers and which has made the job of sales easier by ensuring leads generated align with ideal customers for the firm.

These are all examples of how employees who traditionally didn't consider themselves involved in or supporting sales realized the influence their role can (and should) have on generating new sales. Most importantly, these are all things you can replicate, getting those who directly and indirectly influence your ability to sell involved and shifting toward Team-Based Selling.

Gaining this level of support can be challenging – it can feel like trying to turn a ship. I've had employees tell me they didn't pursue a job in sales, and as a result, they don't desire to interact with customers directly or indirectly.

Fortunately, there's some good news. However monumental, your efforts in this area can and will speed up your sales conversion time and improve your closing ratio. Why? Because you've got *a team* focused on closing the sale, not a lone salesperson who can often feel like they are fighting their own company to close a sale. That's not an environment ripe for multiplying sales.

Here are some best practices you can use to gain and retain the support of the employees outside of sales in your mission to build Team-Based Selling.

SHAWN'S STRATEGIES TO DEVELOP TEAM-BASED SELLING

1. The CEO, President, or General Manager invests time each quarter (at minimum) meeting with customers or potential customers to learn more about their business and their challenges and to identify new opportunities to support customers.
2. As part of the onboarding process for all new employees, individuals spend time with someone in sales "in the field," making customer calls, attending prospect meetings, and understanding the sales process.
3. All department executives and leaders participate in a sales meeting at least once yearly. This can be an annual retreat or a monthly sales meeting, where they gain exposure to challenges, market shifts, new customer opportunities, and more.
4. All managers and front line leaders spend time in sales as part of their ongoing development. They must explain how their team's role directly and indirectly influences their customers to buy, buy more, and buy again.
5. As part of annual performance reviews, all employees must be able to share (in their own words) how their role directly or indirectly influences the customer.

You may only be able to introduce or influence the adoption of a few of these strategies. However, any efforts you place here will only serve to support your sales multiplier formula. In just a moment, I'll explain precisely how.

Recently, we had some problems with our Ford pickup truck. The aging sparkplugs caused drivability problems caused by intermittent issues that left the vehicle low on power. Twice, during two separate trips towing our R.V. trailer, we found ourselves crawling along the shoulder of a highway, limping the truck to our destination. After changing the sparkplugs and seemingly resolving the problem, my wife and I discussed whether to trade it in and look for something newer.

I began researching various brands and models, primarily online, and assessing their available features, towing capacity, fuel mileage, and pricing. Additionally, I spoke with a friend who drives a Dodge Ram and another who drives a newer Ford.

Since we used our truck mainly for towing purposes and had no near-term camping trips planned, there was no urgency to find an alternative. However, as time progressed, we crept closer to a planned trip in August. My wife and I began discussing whether we had seen and resolved the problem with the truck or if we were to find ourselves once again on the side of the road. We even considered canceling the trip in the event additional problems arise. As the sense of urgency increased, I began more intensive research on finding a new truck, looking at various pricing programs, manufacturing incentives, and models in stock at local dealerships.

We narrowed our options down to two different brands and models that were of interest, and after a brief discussion, we decided to contact each dealership to inquire about availability and trade-in value.

I emailed both dealerships with a similar question about the trade-in value of my current Ford pickup. Within 15 minutes, a salesperson from the Ford dealership reached back out to me, answering my email, and asking some additional questions. After an exchange of email and text messages, including pictures of our existing truck, value for the trade-in, and a few unique points shared about the model I was considering, the salesperson emailed me a quote. After reviewing with my wife, I called the salesperson to negotiate additional features and signed the deal.

A salesperson from the second dealer replied to my email the following day around 11 a.m., asking if I'd like to come and see their vehicle (and not answering my question about trade-in value). By then, we had already negotiated with the first dealer and signed back the offer.

If you were to map out the steps that led to our purchase of a new truck, they were as follows:

1. A circumstance that necessitated our investigation into finding a new vehicle.
2. We conducted online research (and some offline) to explore possible options.
3. We socialized our chosen options within our network to gain feedback.
4. A trigger event influenced the timeline and urgency to buy.
5. We requested additional details from the sales professionals to identify our options.
6. We considered the options, contrasting them against our priorities.
7. Then, we negotiated with our selected dealer to identify the best possible outcome.
8. Lastly, we finalized the agreement.

These steps are not unique to buying a new pickup or a Business to Consumer (B2C) sales environment. These are the exact steps your buyers take today when purchasing your product or service, as identified in Figure 4.1.

When considering these steps, the extent to which *employees outside of sales influence the buying decision* may need to be more apparent. For example, look back at some of the steps I outlined above.

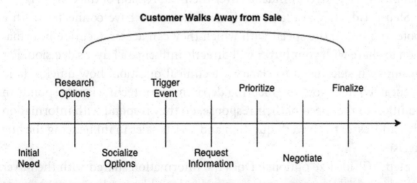

FIGURE 4.1
The Buying Process (Steps listed below – include arrows demonstrating walking away from the deal)

Step 2 (Online research): Most employees post and share information about their company and its products or services on social media. Everything from their employment information shared on LinkedIn to comments mentioned on Facebook or Instagram will appear when customers research online.

Step 3 (Socialize options): Employees discuss their jobs with their network. When they understand and have a positive impression of your company, its products, or services, they share openly when asked about options. What are your employees saying about your company, its products, or services to their friends, family, and extended network? Are they being educated on the value and benefits your product or services bring customers that they can share with their social network?

Step 4 (Trigger event): In some circumstances, your employees can influence trigger events when they understand your products or services' benefits to potential customers. When asked for possible solutions to a circumstance in Step 3, they can share information that is powerful and influential enough that it results in a trigger event. For example, "My company dishwashers offer the best warranty," or "We just won all the delivery business for [insert big company name], so I'm pretty sure we can handle yours as well!"

Step 5 (Request for information): The experience a potential buyer has while reaching out to and requesting information from your company can directly influence their willingness to buy. From how quickly they receive a response to their email or phone message, to whether they are warmly greeted when arriving at your office. Anyone who interacts with a potential buyer has a direct influence over their impression of the company.

Step 6 (Identify available options): Once sales have connected with a potential buyer, the speed with which they can access accurate information to share with your buyer will directly influence a buyer's decision. For example, if sales need to clarify a technical question, how quickly (and accurately) does your engineering department or technicians respond? In addition to the speed of their response, do they respond with information that addresses the buyer's question and assists sales in influencing the buy decision?

Step 7 (Prioritize options): Does the information shared with the buyer by sales, which in many instances is developed by marketing, with input from other departments, focus on sharing benefits and differentiating your product or service in a way that quickly sets you apart from the competition, and other options your buyer might be considering? Further, are you equipping and encouraging all employees who are customer-facing (i.e., customer support, technical support, sales, service, shipping) to collect customer testimonials that sales can share during the sales conversation and that can provide additional credibility and value for your product or service during this stage?

Step 8 (Negotiation best solution): Like step 6, negotiations often require sales to call upon subject matter experts or invite them to join them during the negotiation stage. Do those people or departments recognize what a sound negotiation strategy looks like? Do they realize the influence their personality, words, actions, and the information shared can have on the outcome of the negotiations?

Step 9 (Finalize agreement): A buyer's initial interactions with your company after they have completed negotiations can directly influence whether they remain customers or change their minds. Does everyone in your company know who the new customers are? This allows them to ensure that any information or interaction with this customer is responsive, helpful, and provides a positive experience.

By this point, you should recognize the impact nearly everyone in your company has on your selling ability. As a result, you need to begin shifting toward a more sales-centric culture. Before you do, however, let's consider the message you carry forward, as it can either support or derail your efforts.

ACHIEVING YOUR SALES MULTIPLIER POTENTIAL

Here is a little-known fact you might find interesting. If you are to introduce a highly effective modern sales process, like the one I outline in my book *The Unstoppable Sales Machine: How to Connect, Convert, and Close New Customers*, and then you build a high-performing sales team using the steps I lay out in my book *The Unstoppable Sales Team: Elevate Your Team's Performance, Win More Business, and Attract Top Performers*, you are still not achieving your sales potential. In other words, you can multiply your sales well beyond the methods and strategies I outline in these two books, regardless of the size of your company, the sector you sell into, or the size of your sales team.

STORIES FROM THE SALES FLOOR

Many years ago, I led a small organization with a team of just under 30 staff. As we worked to introduce some of the methods I will share with you in this book, I took the time to meet with each employee to understand their role and their interactions with our customers. In one such meeting, I spoke with Samantha, who coordinated the delivery of services to our customers.

Her role consisted of assisting in drafting emails to our customers, acting as a single point of contact for any customer inquiries about these services, coordinating connections between customers and our program delivery experts, and tracking and monitoring any inquiries, following up as required to determine customer interest. In other words, sales.

My intention was to suggest to Samantha that when she followed up with customers, she could suggest other complimentary services that similar customers had been involved in and found valuable. I call this the "Amazon Effect," taking from the "Other People Who Bought This Product Also Bought" section at the bottom of every Amazon product page. As I explained my idea to Samantha, she stopped me and said, "Listen, if you want me to sell, you're wasting your time. I have nothing to do with sales and want nothing to do with sales."

Samantha's perspective was that she "coordinated" service delivery. She didn't sell. So, I did what any executive faced with the same situation might do: I told her that making this recommendation had nothing to do with selling (umm, it has everything to do with selling) and suggested we make a list of recommended options for her to share with customers.

Weird, I know, but there is a stigma against salespeople. I've been on a mission to reduce the fear of selling, but we'll save that story for another time.

The lesson derived from this encounter was both simple and intriguing at the same time. If your mission is to engage your team in assisting in multiplying your sales, the first thing you'll need to realize is that there is often a stigma or "yuckiness" (as one person in my training program described it) tied to the idea of selling. So, although our intention in the steps I'll be sharing with you is to get everyone in your organization thinking, acting, and behaving like they are in sales, you better refrain from mentioning the word "sales" when you describe what you're doing. It turns some employees off and will make your mission much harder.

For now, let's assume everyone in your organization *is* in sales; they don't know it (and you won't tell them).

YOUR FIRST STEP TOWARD TEAM-BASED SELLING

If everyone is in sales or at least influences your ability to multiply your sales, then you will need to make those people a part of your sales process. Making them a part of your existing sales process makes sense if you have one .... Umm, you do have a proven sales process, don't you? Let's be clear: I'm not talking about CRM software you use to add prospects or manage your pipeline or deal flow. That's an outcome, not an input.

If this is something you don't have in place today, read my book *The Unstoppable Sales Machine: How to Connect, Convert, and Close New Customers.* This book outlines a proven method to sell in the new economy, considering the influences significant events in recent history have had on buying behaviors, from the impact of social media and the rise of AI to increased desires to sell online versus in-person.

Figure 4.2 captures the significant components for building your Unstoppable Sales Machine.

Notice that the outside perimeter highlights four significant components necessary to sell in today's economy, namely:

ATTENTION: Gaining and retaining the attention of your ideal prospects.
CONNECT: Making meaningful contact with your ideal prospects.
ENGAGE: Focusing time, energy, and resources on building trust with your ideal prospects.
SELL: All efforts and energy that sell and serve your prospects continuously.

Sale(s) Opportunity

Gain Attention

Unstoppable Sales™ Machine

Build Engagement

Make Connection

FIGURE 4.2

Unstoppable Sales Machine

These are the primary stages required to make a sale today. Think of it as the first level of influence to generate a sale. By reviewing these levels, one thing should be evident. It requires more than just a salesperson to influence a sale.

In the next section, we will dive deeply into designing and implementing the various components of your sales multiplier formula. Before we do so, however, let me share some perspectives with you. You've likely heard the adage "Don't throw the baby out with the bathwater." The goal of this book, or any of my other books for that matter, is to help you not only raise the bar to sell more but to help you recognize just how far the bar can be raised. The question, then, is whether the efforts warrant the outcomes. Can, for example, you increase the number of upsells or cross-sells you make by involving others and using my serve-and-sell strategy?

Well, that's a good question, but let me ask you: Are you the kind of person who is satisfied with just doing "enough," or do you want to elevate your sales to a level that you are so successful that your peers, your boss, the board, heck even your competition all marvel at your success? I guess if you picked up this book, the short answer is yes.

Here's the good news. You don't need to start from scratch or scrap everything you've accomplished to date to replace it with something new. I will not ask you to throw the baby out with the bathwater. Instead, we'll step through the Sales Multiplier Strategy in stages, allowing you to pick and choose what makes the most sense at this point in your organization's maturity.

However, you must set a few ground rules to get the most from this book.

1. Set achievable objectives. Your goal in introducing the strategies we'll discuss is not to introduce new methods or processes but to create more opportunities to sell, close more sales, and generate more profit. Let these be your guide as to which elements of the strategy you focus your energy and attention on.

2. Set realistic milestones and timelines. Introducing process changes is easy but changing employee behaviors to support those processes can be challenging and take time. As you identify steps you'd like to take, make sure you provide sufficient time for other employees you engage with to adopt and apply these changes. If you don't, you'll become frustrated and likely give up on these strategies.

3. Know when to move on. Although I've seen all the strategies we'll discuss in action and multiplying sales across a wide variety of sectors, not all strategies will be as effective as others. So if you find yourself stuck trying to determine how to introduce some of the strategies we'll discuss, don't stress, just move on to the next one. After all, there is more than one way to skin a cat (apologies to any cat owners; this is just a reference to reinforce the message). Additionally, if you are introducing a strategy and finding it is taking far too long or too much time and energy, park it and move on. You can always return to it later. The goal is to multiply your sales quickly, so you know when to move on.

4. Do more, strategize less. Stay focused on building your strategy. When clients have me onsite for my "Sales Multiplier" workshop, we spend three days, often spread out over some time, to identify the key objectives, measures, and steps to multiply their sales. Although I'm happy, you don't need me to help you do this. But whatever you do, avoid getting stuck making plans and not implementing them. It will be exhausting and disappointing, which is not my intention in writing this book.

Before we discuss the strategies, there is one more consideration that you'll need to make carefully. How can you introduce the Sales Multiplier Strategy to your employees and get them excited and engaged? We'll discuss that and some pointers in the next chapter.

Sales Multiplier Mindset: Most employees have no experience or exposure to sales, and as a result place sales and the customer relationship as the responsibility of someone else (other than themselves). This Sales-Centric Bias is detrimental to your desire to multiply sales.

NOTE

1 https://www.gartner.ca/en/sales/insights/b2b-buying-journey.

Part 2

Your 4.68X Selling Opportunity

The Sales Multiplier Formula provides a method for increasing the size of your sales with every customer. Engaging employees from other departments in applying the framework is recommended but not necessary. In other words, you can introduce the methods we'll discuss without having the full support of others and still see significant increases in multiplying your sales.

In the coming chapters, we'll discuss how you can introduce the sales multiplier framework to achieve 4.68X selling opportunities for every customer you encounter and how to transition from where you are today to achieving significant multipliers in your sales using the sales multiplier framework.

DOI: 10.4324/9781003463962-6

5

The Initial Sale Is Small Potatoes

When I was younger, my first venture into selling was going door to door, introducing myself, and offering my services. The services I provided changed depending on the season. However, the most popular tended to include lawn mowing, deck and fence staining, gardening, and, in the winter, snow shoveling.

My first customer was our next-door neighbor, who approached my parents when I was 11 years old, asking if I could shovel her driveway in the winter months. As spring arrived, I realized that the steady income I had generated from shoveling snow (nearly $5 every time I shoveled it!) was about to come to a complete halt. After getting my parents' approval to use our lawnmower, I offered to mow our neighbor's lawn in the summer. This simple offer doubled the annual income from helping my neighbor as lawns needed to be mowed weekly (and demanded a higher fee). In contrast, snow shoveling depended on the amount of snow we received during the winter months, which varied year over year.

The lawn mowing for my neighbor led to offering additional services such as gardening and staining her deck in the summer months. During the winter, removing snow from her driveway resulted in her being asked periodically to remove the snow from her roof. As other neighbors noticed my services, they also began to ask for my help. One neighbor, for example, who mowed their lawn and shoveled their own driveway, asked if I could assist with shoveling the snow off their roof, which led to their requesting I shovel their driveway while they were away on vacation during the winter months.

At the age of 11, I inadvertently stumbled upon the sales multiplier formula, which helped me increase each customer's Total Customer Sales Value (TCSV) (Figure 5.1).

DOI: 10.4324/9781003463962-7

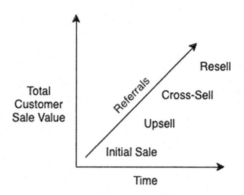

FIGURE 5.1

Introduction of the sales multiplier formula, leading to increase in TCSV

This experience is where my idea for the sales multiplier formula first emerged. For every customer you might sell to, the TCSV is directly related to the products and services you offer. The goal, then, for every customer is to maximize the TCSV, which can be achieved through the sale of additional (and complimentary) products or services. The sales multiplier framework provides you with the method, or framework of sorts, to maximize TCSV for every customer or client.

SELLING OPPORTUNITIES (THAT YOU'RE LIKELY MISSING!)

I'll be the first to admit that while offering additional (and complimentary) services or products to a customer has been around for a while, having a proven framework that focuses intently on increasing the TCSV for every customer is essential. So, how can you get started?

To begin with, consider that for every customer you have today, there is a clear and straightforward path to increasing your sales for that customer by upwards of 4.68 times. You read that correctly. Where does this factor of 4.68 multiplier come from? Well, presuming that you have some additional or complimentary products or services you *can sell* to each customer when appropriately introduced at the right time, you can quickly increase the size of each sale.

Before we dive into how to achieve this multiplier for each customer, let me explain each of the additional selling opportunities you'll pursue to achieve your 4.68 increase in sales.

The Upsell

Opportunity: For every sale you make, there is (or should be) an opportunity to sell the customer into a higher-value package of your products or services. The key to upselling is presenting options to the customer in which the investment is less than the perceived value of the product or service. Automobile manufacturers are infamous for developing upsells that entice their customers to spend more money in return for greater value. When we recently purchased a Ford F150, the options for models included the XL, XLT, XLT, Lariat, Platinum, Limited, and so on.

Examples of Product Upsells:

A higher quality product or premium version of the product.
A similar product that has additional features or benefits.
Additional volume of the product at a lower per-unit price.

Examples of Service Upsells:

Complimentary services bundled with an existing service.
An extended service period.
A similar service with additional benefits or outcomes.

Challenge: The opportunity to make an upsell is an immediate opportunity to increase the TCSV of your clients or customers. Unfortunately, if you leave the upsell opportunity up to the customer (to understand, uncover, and decide upon), you are missing out on over 80% of upsell opportunities. There are several reasons for this missed opportunity, starting with the fact that you may need to position the offering in a way that is appealing to your customer or client. Since this is quite common, let me explain why.

We've all experienced an upsell that could have been a better fit from the offer you received to add a warranty to what is essentially a throw-away electronic item, a recommendation to buy the overpriced undercoating for a vehicle you're planning to lease, or the offer to indulge in a decadent dessert after you've already filled up on the main course. These experiences make us sensitive to anyone who attempts to upsell us. As a result, we can often react negatively or even walk away from a deal when offered something that appears to take advantage of us.

Every salesperson has experienced this kind of challenge at one point or another. If they've been selling for more than a year, they've likely even lost a deal to a potential customer after having presented an upsell that wasn't a good fit. This leads to most sales professionals shying away from the upsell, either for fear of losing a deal or not having the skills to assess what upsells are a good fit and how they can best be presented.

Solution: In many instances, upsells are best introduced *after the initial sale*, in which case the relationship (and the sale) is already secured, and any risks of upsetting the customer or losing the sale have diminished. Do you return to the customer after the initial sale to attempt to make an upsell? My experience suggests that this is not the case. Departments outside sales can initiate upsells if they are engaged with your customers or clients. If this isn't possible, you need to have a follow-up method with all new customers, including presenting upsell options. Here is where your real upsell opportunity exists.

The Cross-Sell

Opportunity: A cross-sell involves approaching an existing customer with a different product or service to sell them. In some instances, these may be complimentary (e.g., you recently purchased some mutual funds from us, and we wanted to offer you an opportunity to open a high-interest savings account) or not (e.g., you recently purchased a new SUV from us, and our Harley Davidson division is having a special on new Street Glides).

Where an Upsell focuses on increasing a customer's investment, a Cross-Sell focuses on using existing customers as leads for other, sometimes dissimilar, products or services.

Examples of Product Cross-Sells:

A product that is complimentary.
A product that is not complimentary.

Examples of Service Cross-Sells:

A service that is complimentary.
A service that is not complimentary.

Challenge: In a cross-sell situation, you often approach existing customers (or prospects) with a different product or service to sell, so timing and positioning can be key to successful cross-selling. In other words, cross-sells are often more difficult to make because of positioning the new product or service and, as a result, require some strategic positioning to be effective.

Unfortunately, however, many of the sales professionals I've met do not enjoy cross-selling for the very same reason they don't enjoy upselling. They view the customer relationship as delicate and are highly sensitive (and somewhat hesitant) to approach a customer and offer to sell them something different for fear of losing trust and a future opportunity to sell.

Solution: By focusing your efforts on identifying the best options, timing, and positioning of your cross-sells, you make the introduction of cross-sells easier and create both interest (on the part of your customer) and accountability (for yourself) to follow up. Moreover, when you engage other departments in supporting your cross-selling efforts, you further increase your chances of making a cross-selling.

Let's look at some examples:

Customer Service hears a customer complain about a different supplier for which your company (or one of its divisions) has products or services.

Reception has a brief chat with a customer who calls in frequently and learns the customer is having an issue in an area that your company has products or services to resolve.

Shipping calls a customer to book delivery and learns of the customer having issues with scheduling carriers, for which your company has services that support or provide improved logistics.

Operations speaks with a customer and learns the customer is having difficulty retaining their employees. Your company offers additional products or services, which could eliminate the need for the customer to hire more employees.

In each of these examples, employees outside of sales can assist you in identifying and possibly even positioning a cross-sell opportunity, setting you up for an easier conversation and an easier close.

The Resell

Opportunity: A resell is what it sounds like. It is the act of reselling an existing customer or client on purchasing the same product or service they've already invested in, sometimes repeatedly.

Depending on your product or service, the duration of reselling your customer or client may vary. For example, selling capital equipment in high volumes may result in a less frequent resell opportunity than operating a restaurant and convincing patrons to return for the same meal the next day.

Examples of Product Resells:

Negotiate a new contract or new term for purchasing the same product.

Re-purchase the same product (with the same price, volume, and terms).

Introduce a new agreement to purchase the same product (different price, volume, or terms).

Example of Service Resells:

Negotiate a renewal of an existing service contract or agreement.

Re-purchase the same service (terms, options, and price).

Negotiate a new agreement for the same service (different terms, options, and price).

Challenge: Resell opportunities can be easy for sales to close, but the problem lies herein. Easy sales often result in little effort on our (sales) part. After all, if they seem happy, why put that much effort into the sale? In my work with companies globally, I've repeatedly found that most customer relationships transition from the salesperson (who initiates and nurtures the relationship) to other key employees with whom a customer interacts frequently. Although resells are typically something sales are comfortable pursuing and effective in closing, we must consider to what extent others should be involved and where it makes sense to get them involved.

In some instances, several obstacles can result in not being successful in making a resell, for example:

Losing track of the timing of the resell and not following up, resulting in losing the resell.

Disengagement during the product or service delivery, resulting in a loss of customer relationship and a challenge in making the resell.

Changes in key relationships (i.e., buyer) during the service term or product delivery, resulting in sales having to start fresh with building relationships for the resell (meanwhile, other employees have remained engaged with these new contacts).

Solution: Relationships for resells are often transferred from sales to other departments during product or service delivery. When this happens, those other departments become integral to the customer relationship. They can usually provide critical insights that can assist on determining when to introduce the resell or any adjustments in positioning or timing to secure the sale.

You might think this information is being transferred to sales when appropriate, but after nearly two decades of working with sales teams and leaders, I've learned that this is only sometimes the case. In many instances, you must be in a better position to succeed at a resell. Although you should remain part of the process, involving other departments who engage with the customer regularly is a much better and more effective approach.

The upsell, cross-sell, and resell are only a part of your 4.68X selling opportunity and are significant components of your Sales Multiplier Formula. We'll discuss these in greater depth and the other formula elements shortly. Let's discuss how to maximize each of these selling opportunities. If you only implement this part of the sales multiplier formula and do so effectively, you'll experience a significant increase in sales. However, achieving this increase requires considering some crucial aspects of your sales methods.

CLOSING SHOULD BE A TEAM SPORT

Building on our discussions around Team-Based Selling, closing a deal is no exception to this rule. Unfortunately, however, it's easy for sales professionals to become fixated on closing new deals to generate sales, instead of considering how to expand the size of every sale with each customer you encounter. In other words, don't be so quick to move on to the next selling opportunity after you close the initial deal. Instead, consider how you can mine each of your customers to extract more selling opportunities.

When you assess every prospect or customer interaction as an opportunity to upsell, cross-sell, or even resell, the view on the total value of each customer shifts. Additionally, if you were to consider each existing customer as a source of unstoppable referrals, well, again your perspective on what each customer relationship can mean in terms of sales suddenly changes.

There's one problem, however. For many sales professionals, the idea of spending precious time mining existing customers means less time spent on direct selling activities and searching for new prospects, which is a problem. The solution, in my experience, is getting others in your company onboard to support *closing* your selling opportunities.

Let me explain.

Closing is a sales discipline in and of itself that requires skills, expertise, and effort. If you've identified a new opportunity and engaged the prospect in your sales process, can you (or should you) wash your hands and walk away from the latest customer once they've closed? The short answer is no. The sale may be lost if you step away from the customer relationship at this critical juncture.

If you've ever contacted a credit card company with questions about your account or about changing your credit limit, then it's likely that you've been asked to participate in a survey at the end of the call. This is usually a sales pitch in disguise, where you are offered the chance to make a one-time purchase of a great deal on a vacation, insurance, or otherwise. You only need to sit through one of these never to want to do so again. If you still need to sit through one of these, think of it like a timeshare pitch. If you can sit through the pitch, you'll receive a gift at the end of the presentation (typically regardless of whether you buy or not).

When we form a relationship with someone, even after a brief interaction or discussion, and then attempt to transition that relationship to someone else, we diminish trust. Like sitting through the credit card presentation or the timeshare pitch, our instincts suggest that "someone is going to try and sell us something, so let's get out of here!"

TRUST CAN'T BE TRANSFERRED

As a result, instead of running away or stepping out after you make a sale, you should stick around in support of closing new opportunities. This isn't to say you need to manage the account and be involved in every customer discussion or decision, but you also don't want to drop them like a wet noodle.

Additionally, suppose an employee who works closely with an existing customer identifies a potential opportunity with that customer. In that case, they should remain part of the sales process moving forward, not just

Customer Sale Journey

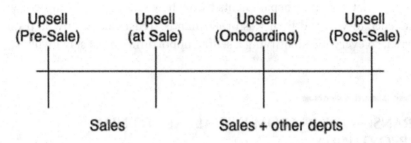

FIGURE 5.2
Existing customer opportunity and employee involvement as sales weaves in and out of the interaction through to close

disappear after they turn the opportunity over to sales (I call this the dump and run!). Your customers seek a company that meets their needs and takes a collaborative approach. They don't want to feel like they are being sold, and a dump and run suggests just that. Figure 5.2 demonstrates the opportunity.

Let's look at an example. Suppose someone on your Customer Service team learns of a new customer requirement that your company can support. They arrange a meeting between themselves, the customer, and you (in sales) to discuss what the customer has shared (i.e., the opportunity). They share their understanding of the situation with you, asking the customer to confirm. Following this validation, you likely dive more deeply with the customer, asking questions to confirm understanding and the opportunity. Once your discussion is complete, sales will recommend the next steps. If the debate were straightforward (i.e., the customer is seeking something your upsell or cross-sell can offer), customer service would typically remain in the meeting. If, however, it will take a more in-depth conversation (i.e., more complex, or high cost upsell), they might possibly excuse themselves, circling back with the customer at the end of the call or meeting to ensure the opportunity was addressed to their satisfaction.

In this example, customer service is the person with the relationship and, as a result, should remain involved in the discussion (and sales process), dramatically increasing both the likelihood of the sale being made and the speed at which it is closed.

Suppose you want to capitalize on your 4.68X selling opportunity. In that case, you handle the close BUT ensure anyone who interacted with the customer or client remains a part of the closing process. Whatever you do, don't let the other departments throw new selling opportunities over the fence to you and then wash their hands. Trust can't easily be transferred, so everyone identifying a selling opportunity must stay involved.

TRANSITIONING FROM INITIAL SALE TO NEW OPPORTUNITY

You may be wondering, how do we transition from my making the initial sale to a customer to capturing these additional selling opportunities when I'm not fully plugged into everything our customers say and do with the rest of the organization? Does the idea of having a culture that serves and sells your customers mean that sales should refrain from offering upsells or attempting a cross-sell when the opportunity arises? Of course, not; there is no need to change what you're doing today, presuming they have the right skills and ability to present an upsell or cross-sell when appropriate.

The "opportunity" to increase your sales with existing and new customers or clients arises when you equip others who interact with customers with the skills and confidence to recognize, position, and initiate new sales opportunities, most often in the form of upsells, cross-sells, and resells. Before we dive into the steps to introduce the sales multiplier formula, let's explore some frequently asked questions I receive when introducing this model into your organization.

INTRODUCING THE SALES MULTIPLIER FORMULA: FREQUENTLY ASKED QUESTIONS

How does an employee outside the sales department recognize a new selling opportunity?

Most employees don't recognize a selling opportunity because they've never been asked to recognize such a situation. When you hire someone in customer service, customer support, accounts receivable, or operations, for example, it is unlikely you are looking for someone with the attributes of a good salesperson. Additionally, these employees have often yet to be exposed to the idea of being involved in the sales process.

When you introduce the ideas shared in this book, you'll find that most employees have no real issue with becoming part of the sales process if you don't make it an expectation that they will make a sale (earlier, we discussed why this is).

We'll dive into the specifics of how to get each employee in these different departments on board in the upcoming chapters. For now, just know that you'll use specific strategies; some will be global and applied to all staff, and others will be specific to each department.

Does the employee make the sale?

The short answer is no; however, there is a caveat. You will find that some employees, regardless of their department, are good at and comfortable asking for the sale. For these employees, you'll want to explore whether allowing them to make the sale makes sense.

For example, someone in reception asking a customer for a sale may be inappropriate, whereas equipping customer service or customer support with the skills and ability to ask for the sale may make sense. The critical question is whether you allow an employee to ask for the sale: "Does it make sense to the customer that this employee asks for the sale?" Avoid it if it seems awkward; otherwise, it's okay.

Is there a hand-off to the sales department of some kind?

Yes. The Selling Opportunity method will equip you and your team with the triggers, skills, scripts, and procedures to identify the sale, know when to involve the sales department, and, most importantly, how to bring sales into the conversation.

Two factors must be considered to ensure an effective hand-off results in a sale. First, the transition must seem like a natural evolution to the customer. The goal is to make this as fluid and natural for the customer as possible (as discussed earlier). As crucial as the hand-off is the follow-up. Clear responsibility for who will follow up and when will ensure that new selling opportunities identified and passed along to sales are fully capitalized on. The follow-up can be done by either the sales department or the employee who made the connection. We'll discuss how in future chapters.

Do all my employees need to sit in sales meetings?

The short answer is no. However, for the record, I recommend that your employees who are involved in the selling opportunity method gain some exposure to the sales department, its goals, challenges, methods, and strategies. Doing so will educate others on what the sales department focuses on and the value it brings to the organization.

Exposing other departments to a periodic sales meeting also helps build faster engagement in the selling opportunity. It can also overcome barriers that can present themselves in the form of jealousy (or frustration) by departments that don't have the same freedoms as sales (i.e., not being in the office every day, traveling during company time).

Is this restricted to some employees, or is everyone involved?

The Selling Opportunity engages everyone across the organization. The goal is to build awareness among all employees of their role in identifying and supporting new selling opportunities. You may involve only specific departments that interact with your customers regularly. These departments commonly include customer service, customer support, accounts receivable, logistics, and shipping.

How do I convince employees outside the sales department to get involved in the selling opportunity?

You'll need to use some specific methods to build awareness and acceptance of the Selling Opportunity method. We'll discuss how to do this in future chapters. For now, consider that the most valuable role you can play is to consistently discuss the selling opportunity every chance you get.

For example, point out opportunities outside of sales to others, recommend that other departments attend a sales meeting, and share sales wins that involve different departments during town halls.

With these questions out of the way, let's dive into the specifics of your sales multiplier formula by discussing the good, better, and best approach to generating additional sales.

Sales Multiplier Mindset: For every customer that you have today, there is a clear and straightforward path to increasing your sales for that customer by upwards of 4.68 times.

6

Good: Every Good Sale Deserves an Upsell

Whether you are a sales professional, a sales executive or leader, or an entrepreneur, you can (and should) multiply your sales using what I refer to as the "Good, Better, Best" Approach to Selling. This approach is a formula for multiplying your sales' size and frequency.

Additionally, it's not just the steps I'm going to lay out that will multiply your sales; it's the sequence, the frequency, and the consistency with which you practice the steps that will result in higher and more frequent sales. For this reason, don't let yourself dismiss a chapter or section because you think you've already "got it." There are so many tiny nuances that I will share that can have a dramatic impact on your sales outcomes.

THE GOOD, BETTER, BEST APPROACH TO SELLING

When my boys bring home their report cards from school, they follow a considerably different format from my years in grade school. When I was younger, report cards used a letter grade to identify a student's progress using the following scale:

A = Excellent
B = Very Good
C = Satisfactory
D = Needs Improvement
F = Fail

DOI: 10.4324/9781003463962-8

Although grading on report cards may have changed over the years, generally, they still follow a structure of labeling performance at a minimum of four levels:

Excellent
Good
Satisfactory
Needs Improvement

Under this grading system, moving from Needs Improvement up, a student doesn't comprehend what they are being taught, barely understands it, understands it, or fully comprehends it.

If you were to apply this simplified grade structure to your ability to fully capitalize on each (and every) selling opportunity with your existing customers or clients, what grade would you select? In my experience, your sales would likely fall into Good, Satisfactory, or Needs Improvement for the following reasons:

1. Needs Improvement: Your sales are below your expectations or needs, and you desperately need ideas and methods to increase them.
2. Satisfactory: Your sales are satisfactory; however, you are just covering expenses and need to generate more sales to grow your company.
3. Good: Your sales are already good, but you like generating more sales without hiring more people.

With what I will lay out in this book, I'd suggest your sales are satisfactory at best. Even if you have an effective process for selling in today's market (like the one I outline in my book *The Unstoppable Sales Machine*), a top-performing sales team (like the one described in my book *The Unstoppable Sales Team*), or significant market share, there is still considerable room to generate more sales with your existing customers, prospects, and even past customers (and there's an example of one of those nuances I mentioned. … Are you repeatedly selling to your past customers? More to come here).

Even the highest-performing sales professionals often miss out on additional selling opportunities that can dramatically increase the TCRV.

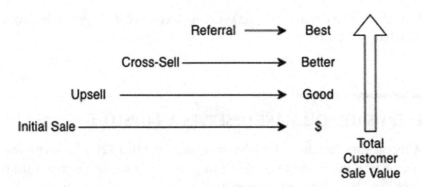

FIGURE 6.1
Diagram showing the good, better, and best approach

Good = Generating upsell opportunities.
Better = Generating both upsell and cross-sell opportunities.
Best = Generating upsell, cross-sell, and referral opportunities.

These have nothing to do with the initial sale but rather the extra sales possible for each customer using the Good, Better, Best approach to selling, as identified in Figure 6.1.

Before we discuss how you'll increase the size of every sale, let's take a moment to consider some critical points we've discussed thus far, as it pertains to your approach to sales (and your perspective on multiplying sales).

1. Each customer you sell to today is NOT a single sales opportunity but a series of selling opportunities that progress in value, size, and revenue.
2. These additional selling opportunities often run in parallel, not serial.
3. Uncovering these selling opportunities requires a broader perspective than your sales department can share.
4. Closing these additional selling opportunities requires each one to be identified, developed, and nurtured before they can close (in other words, they won't close themselves!).
5. The only way to fully uncover and close these additional selling opportunities is to apply a formula that complements your existing sales process and engages your broader team of employees.

Now that we've covered this, let's discuss a good selling approach – your Upsell opportunity!

EVERY SALE YOU MAKE DESERVES AN UPSELL

A recent study conducted by HubSpot suggested that 72% of sales professionals who upsell say that 30% of their company's revenue comes from upselling.[1] In other words, if done well, done right, and done consistently, a 30% boost in revenue is possible just through upselling alone.

The concept of upselling is not new. What is new, however, is the idea that your prospect should always have upsell options to choose from. You've likely heard the saying, "For every action, there is an equal and opposite reaction." Well, from now on, I want you to remember that "for every sale, there is a higher-valued and higher-priced upsell."

Ensuring every customer sale consists of sharing upsell options is one of the fastest and easiest ways to increase the TCSV we discussed earlier. More importantly, upsell options can help to close the sale, as they transition your prospect from thinking, "Do I buy this or not?" to "Which option is best for me?"

Let's begin with a definition to clarify what I mean by saying "upsell." An upsell is a different product or service perceived as being of higher value by your prospect or customer. There are two types of upsells. First is a product or service that exists on its own (stand-alone upsell) and complements the core offering. Alternatively, an upsell can be a product or service that provides additional features or benefits that can be added to or included with the original product or service (add-on upsell).

The best practice is to have a combination of higher-value products to point the prospect toward and a series of options that can slowly and incrementally build the product or service's value.

Example of a stand-alone upsell:

1. Convincing a customer to buy a different and more expensive furnace.
2. Persuading a customer to order a higher-priced lawnmower.
3. Compelling a client to move to a higher-service package (for more money).

Example of add-on upsells:

4. Convincing customers to add more options to their new vehicle (i.e., rust protection).
5. Compelling a customer to increase the volume of their shipment.
6. Persuading a client to extend their retainer.

There is a process for effectively presenting an upsell to a customer. If you expect to persuade the customer to invest, it takes skill in timing and language to share and recommend an upgraded product, additional features, or a more robust service. We'll discuss the best way to make this presentation in a moment.

Here is one of those moments when you might be thinking, "No problem, Shawn, I'm well-versed and skilled in presenting upsell options, so I'll just skip ahead." Well, here's the thing you might have yet to consider. The upsell is often something a customer or client seriously considers *after making the initial buy decision.* Therefore, you have two options. Either involve other departments or individuals as part of your upsell process (interacting with your prospects during these times) or strategically follow up with every customer post-sale at the right times to position the upsell.

What I've found in my work with sales and customer service teams from around the globe is that when it comes to making upsells, every organization falls into one of three main categories:

1. There is a wide variety of upsell options (stand-alone and add-ons) for your customers:
   a. Pro: There are options you can draw upon to move customers to a higher-valued (and higher-priced) option.
   b. Con: You may have too many options to determine the best option for the customer.
   c. Con: You may not be in the right place to recommend or secure the upsell at the right time.
   d. Con: Many sales professionals are timid to introduce upsells as they deem them as threatening to secure the sale.
2. There are limited upsell options for your customers:
   a. Pro: Depending on the customer's purchases, an upsell option may not exist.

    b. Con: Every purchase does not present an upsell opportunity; hence, the revenue potential of each customer is limited.

    c. Con: You may not be able to offer an upsell in every "buy" situation, and as a result forget to offer even existing upsells when the opportunity arises.

3. There are no upsell options for your customers:

    a. Pro: ... To be honest, I'm struggling to write something here!

    b. Con: You are missing out on a significant opportunity to increase the value of every sale with your customers.

    c. Con: You are not accustomed to or equipped with the skills to upsell.

Depending on which of these three categories you fall in, it's easy to see where you need to make improvements if you want to capitalize on your upsell opportunity. Additionally, what is missing from above is the fact that upsell opportunities can exist at three different stages in the customer relationship as shown in Figure 6.2.

You can see from this figure that if you want to fully capitalize on your upsell opportunity, you need to expand both the awareness of upsell options as well as educate others in your organization as to the trigger points for when upsells may be a good option to present.

I mentioned earlier my experience selling cars at a young age, during which time I worked very closely with several "service advisors." While delivering a new car to a customer, I would often introduce them to an advisor, so they knew who to contact for service. Doing so increased services ability to gain a customer (not everyone services their vehicle at the

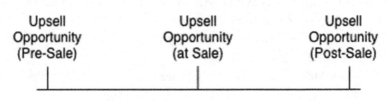

Customer Sale Journey

| Upsell Opportunity (Pre-Sale) | Upsell Opportunity (at Sale) | Upsell Opportunity (Post-Sale) |

FIGURE 6.2

Upsell at pre-sale, upsell at sale, and upsell post-sale

dealership). In return, the service would send existing customers to consider buying a new car in my direction. I capitalized on this relationship with service on a much deeper level, educating them and gaining their support in presenting upsell options to customers. For example, as I turned the customer over to service if we had discussed an extended warranty, undercoating, or other "upsell" options, I would mention this during the turnover. Here is an example of the dialogue:

> John, please meet Susan, our Service Advisor. Susan, I wanted to introduce you to John, who is purchasing a new Buick Enclave. We discussed how expensive parts for repairs can be, so John is considering whether an extended warranty would make sense. What are your thoughts?

As you might imagine, Susan and I had discussed the various upsell options, and the language I used in my turnover of John to Susan (which was her opportunity to begin building a relationship with John for service business) flagged her to first discuss the upsell and its benefits. Susan would often agree with my point, and "recommend" this as a wise decision to John.

If I hadn't educated Susan on the various upsell options and we hadn't come up with a clear method for partnering on presenting upsells, then the upsell itself would have had a lesser chance of happening.

In this example, I took the steps to partner with someone outside sales to influence upsell options. So, don't get hung up on the idea that this needs to be a company or at least a sales-driven initiative. You can develop individual relationships with those who interact with your customers, helping them adopt simple steps or scripts that can dramatically increase your upsell options.

Now, can you imagine if the dealer principal had done this intentionally? Can you imagine the impact on TCRV?[2]

When you intentionally educate others who interact with your customers or clients on recognizing and influencing upsell opportunities, your chances of making an upsell increase exponentially! Educating your employees outside the sales department on upsell opportunities (and their benefits to the customer) is essential, but that's only one part of the equation. They also need to understand the skills to position the upsell, enabling sales, or possibly themselves, to close it. With this in mind, let's discuss positioning upsells next.

FIVE UPSELL OPPORTUNITIES FOR EVERY CUSTOMER

Recognizing when an upsell opportunity first presents itself helps inform who is best to present the presentation. Commonly, the upsell is thought of as something that can only happen at the time of the sale, for example:

Product Example: Your customer selects a product to buy at a specific volume, and sales suggest increasing the volume to a higher level, which would help them achieve a price discount (e.g., purchasing 500 instead of 250 to get a small reduction on the per-unit price).

Service Example: A client selects a service to buy, and sales suggests they consider the following "package," which contains this service, as well as several other features that could benefit them.

Whatever the situation, an upsell can exist at multiple points in your customer or client journey, as demonstrated by Figure 6.3.

Upsell Opportunity #1: Consideration (Timeline: Post Initial Discovery Meeting)

At the consideration stage, your prospect is considering your offer and is undecided about what to invest in. This is a stage upon which sales commonly make recommendations around upsells, building on the benefits the prospect is seeking and demonstrating an increased return on

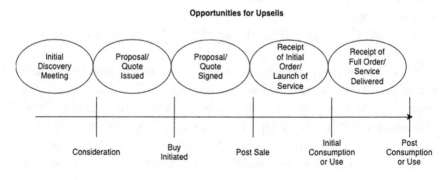

FIGURE 6.3

The various points at which an upsell can be introduced

investment (ROI). If you involve other departments in this early stage, it's important that they understand what upsell options exist and how to present them.

Here are some examples:

The prospect speaks with Engineering about their product design or features.

The prospect interacts with a technician to diagnose their circumstances.

Prospects frequently connect with customer service as a first point of contact.

Upsell Opportunity #2: Buy Initiated (Timeline: Proposal or Quote Issued)

During this stage, your prospect has completed their initial research and discussions and is now ready to "buy" your product or service. Sales is often the primary contact at this point and will present the upsell options before and during the close.

Sometimes, you may need to involve other departments (or the prospect will speak with other departments). Therefore, several different departments should be made aware of upsell options. Additionally, since you are about to close a new customer, it's important that others who may interact with this prospect (soon-to-be customer or client) are made aware the prospect is considering moving forward so that they can interact with the prospect in a way that supports closing the deal. It's not uncommon for prospects to reach out to those internally with whom they've met or spoken with questions before deciding whether to proceed.

Here are some examples:

Reception is made aware the prospect is considering moving forward when responding to the prospect's inbound call and shares their "excitement" at the prospect considering working with the company.

Customer service is made aware of the potential for the prospect to close; they are prepared to discuss potential upsell options if the prospect reaches out to them with any questions or clarifications.

Departments involved in the earlier "consideration" stage are aware of the potential for close (i.e., Engineering, technical design) and are prepared if the prospect contacts them with additional follow-up questions.

Upsell Opportunity #3: Post Sale (Timeline: Contract or Agreement Signed)

However, after the sale is complete before the ink dries, it is a great opportunity to engage the customer in an upsell. Studies have repeatedly shown that with so much new information prospects receive daily, it can take a long time to decide to buy. Moreover, once the decision is made, there is a chance that the customer will have second thoughts as new information arises. Don't let this concern you; instead, use this to your advantage! Consider this a chance to present upsells, which can add further value to the sale to the prospect. It's crucial at this stage to recognize who will interact with the client during the first 24, 48, and 72 hours post-close and then to equip them with various upsell options, scripts, and resources that they might need to recommend an upsell.

Here are some examples:

Accounts Receivable reaches out to the (now) customer with their first invoice; they should recognize upsell options if there are questions about the amount invoiced or payment terms. Upsells can be positioned as "beneficial" if the value of the upsells outweighs the perceived cost.

Customer Service is often the first point of contact post-sale for onboarding or introduction; like the "Buy Initiated" stage, they should be aware of upsell options and be positioned to recommend and secure upsells. You can do this assertively, "I'm surprised you didn't go with our deluxe package," or passively, "You mention you are planning to place another order next month; if we bundle these together, I think I can get you a discount. Would you like me to look into this for you?"

Technical Support reaches out to the prospect to discuss the project, and the customer shares some ideas about further support or assistance. Technical support must be clear on what additional services and/or packages were discussed and are still feasible, and in turn, it must be able to mention these and direct the client in the event this is something that (still) might be of interest.

Upsell Opportunity #4: Initial Receipt (Timeline: Receipt of Initial Order or Launch of Service)

Once the customer or client has received the product or engaged in the service, it is an opportunity to make an upsell. At this point, payment is often only occasionally accepted, and therefore, the chance to increase the value of the sale exists. Presuming you've built some excitement and anticipation with the customer about using the product or experiencing the results of the service (you have done this, right?), it's the best time to build upon the initial excitement by presenting upsell options.

Capitalizing on this upsell opportunity once the initial product or service has been received requires that you have three things in place:

1. For every product or service, there must be clear upsell options that can act as an order add-on or Improvement to the order (i.e., undercoating to a new car can be applied after delivery but at a price discussed during the deal; the additional insurance coverage can be added even though the policy has been initiated).
2. The upsell "add-on" options build upon the initial product or service and improve its condition.
3. Your processes must allow these to be "added" to an order or contract once initiated (i.e., an additional product can be shipped with the next shipment, or extra features can be added to the service).

Examples of Upsells once a contract or project has been initiated:

Project Management recognizes potential upsell options or add-ons and is confident in their ability to make recommendations when customer or client demands in the early stages of the agreement would be best served by moving to a higher option or adding additional stages to the project.

Account Managers are aware of potential upsell options or add-ons. They can suggest to clients that they move up a package or add features when they would add value to the engagement and improve the client's overall experience.

Production is aware of possible upsell options for the order (i.e., higher-quality product to be introduced, increased volume shipped, increased number of quality checks) AND can make these as recommended changes to the existing contract and not simply include them under the existing agreement.

Upsell Opportunity #5: Post Sale (Timeline: Upon receipt of order or delivery of service)

A post-sale upsell is sometimes possible and highly depends on your product or service. The key, however, to this upsell is that once an agreement or contract has been initiated, sales will often move on to the next prospect, leaving other departments to maintain the customer or client relationship. In this situation, the power and influence over the relationship often transition; hence, sales must be in the strongest position to make subsequent sales.

Educating those departments and individuals who engage with customers after the initial sale on upsell options allows them the ability and confidence to plant seeds for the customer's next order. Several years ago, when we purchased a new baseball bat for my oldest son, we decided on a "budget-level" bat. We stopped by the same sports store during the season, and the attendant, clearly recognizing my son, asked how the bat was working out. My son mentioned it seemed a bit heavier than some of the other players' bats, to which the attendant immediately responded by suggesting that he consider a new bat at the end of the season when the sales were on (and to ensure he connected on more pitches in the next season).

Examples of Upsells Post Sale:

Customer Service is aware of additional features or upsell packages and their differences. As they get to know the client or customer, they identify situations during which the next-level package or add-on features would make for a better experience for the client or customer. This information can be mentioned and logged in the CRM for future discussion with the customer.

Accounts Receivable learns that the client prefers to take an early payment discount, which validates the availability of funds. It shares this with sales as a prompt to be more assertive on the upsell during the next purchase (as there is likely more budget available).

Account Managers learn more intimate details about the client's business and are best positioned to make recommendations on "moving up" in their package or service at renewal time to reap the additional benefits they'll receive.

Notice that at virtually every stage described above, the sales department needs to be in a better position of influence over making an upsell. They are part of the equation for sure; however, as I shared earlier, they are sometimes in a better position to present the upsell options or add-ons.

Additionally, upsells are NOT limited to only at the time of sale but rather extend from pre- to post-sale. As a result, having a wide variety of upsell options and add-ons increases your chance of closing the upsell.

If there is anything you've gleaned from above, it should be this. You have five distinct opportunities upon which to offer an upsell. Each of these opportunities involves different members of your team, all of whom can assist in suggesting, recommending, and sharing information about the upsell. Lastly, these opportunities exist before, during, and even after your prospect decides to buy.

Knowing your upsell opportunities and who is best involved is one part of the equation. However, there is still the question of how to best position each prospect for an upsell. Positioning is, after all, the secret to ensuring that you have the greatest opportunity to close the upsell. Here are my Five Rules for Positioning Your Upsell to offer you the greatest chances of closing the deal.

SHAWN'S FIVE RULES FOR POSITIONING EFFECTIVE UPSELLS

Rule #1: Upsell opportunities are identified for each stage of the prospect-to-customer journey.

Rule #2: Every employee must clearly understand what upsell opportunities exist and how they can best support and position them.

Rule #3: There are clear incentives to entice customer-facing, non-sales roles to engage in and support upsell opportunities to the greatest extent possible.

Rule #4: There are additional incentives (i.e., commissions, bonuses) to close upsell opportunities.

Rule #5: Clear measures track the status of upsell opportunities for each stage and for every prospect, customer, or client.

If you ensure these five rules are in place for every prospect who enters your sales pipeline, your chances of closing an upsell increase substantially. In my experience, the success rate of closing upsells increases by more than 50%. This number still moves higher when the upsells have been designed in a way that is complementary to your offer and presents a significant return on your customer or client's investment.

Additionally, having a formula in place for presenting and closing upsells, one that is understood, applied, and supported by all employees, dramatically increases your ability to close upsells and differentiate your offer from the competition, allowing you to charge more. That's right! As you increase the TCSV, you further increase the brand equity of your product, service, and company because what you offer is different from the competition and complimentary to resolving your customer's or client's issues. As a result, you can charge more for what you sell! Are you starting to see why this is a Sales *Multiplier* Formula?

Before we go any deeper, however, let's take a minute to discuss one of the most significant steps in your upsell system that often gets overlooked.

The most significant risk you face when capitalizing on your newly minted upsell system is ensuring that each upsell opportunity is followed through. As your list of prospects and customers increases, so do the number of stages to track, manage, and implement using your upsell system described above. Even if another employee assists you by initially suggesting an upsell to the customer, the upsell won't close itself. In most circumstances, this will set the stage for an upsell, which will require a follow-up, if not several follow-ups.

Let's look at an example of what an upsell opportunity may look like for a single prospect and how quickly the follow-ups and activity can mount.

YOUR UPSELL FOLLOW-UP SYSTEM IN ACTION

Stage 1: Consideration:

Goal: Track upsell discussions for future reference and addition to a quote or proposal.

Stage 2: Buy Initiated:

Goal: Track upsell discussions or suggestions and share them with sales for immediate follow-up.

Stage 3: Post Sale:

Goal: Track upsell discussions or suggestions and share them with sales for future follow-up.

Stage 4: Initial Consumption:

Goal: Track upsell recommendations and share them with sales for future follow-up (new orders, sales).

Stage 5: Post Consumption:
Goal: Track upsell recommendations and share with sales for future orders or needs.

More follow-ups mean more steps in your sales process. Moreover, as follow-ups for each Upsell opportunity begin, the number of follow-ups you need to track and manage will increase quickly. Follow-up will often require a team effort (those who initiated the upsell, as well as sales), and considering the number of other activities you are involved in, it will be easy to lose track of all the upsell opportunities created.

To avoid this from happening (and upsell opportunities slipping away), organize additional stages in your sales pipeline to help you track the upsells. You can set this up in your database (e.g., CRM software, Excel spreadsheet, whatever works!) and develop new steps for each customer to progress through. Use the stages I listed above as examples.

As follow-ups are presented to a customer or client, set a date for the next stage of follow-up. Any good CRM software will allow you to set reminders on dates and times to follow up, but it is optional. (I've seen some elaborate follow-up systems handled through a combination of Excel and Outlook.)

The key to fully capitalizing on your upsell system is to follow up, follow up, and follow up. Track this closely, and you'll be on your way to dramatically increasing upsells.

At this point, we've only just begun multiplying your sales. In the next chapter, let's move from Good (Upsells) to something even better (insert suspenseful music here).

Exciting, right?

Sales Multiplier Mindset: For every prospect, customer, or client you encounter, there are five upsell opportunities you can capitalize on.

NOTES

1 https://blog.hubspot.com/sales/upselling-vs-downselling
2 Note: In automotive sales, upsells outside of the sales department persuasion typically fall to the Finance Manager, whose job is to upsell you with add-ons such as rust protection and extended warranty.

7

Better: Introduce Creative Cross-Selling

Recently, my youngest son and I visited a new fast-food restaurant in our local area. It's a privately owned restaurant operated from its original location, about an hour from our home, for nearly twenty years. Fortunately for us, they decided to open a second location only twenty minutes from our house. Since I had to drive my oldest son to a hockey practice in the same town around dinner time, it was the perfect opportunity for us to try the new location out.

As we placed our orders, the young lady behind the counter offered us French fries and a drink and suggested ice cream for dessert, all great examples of cross-sells. She sold us the drink but not the dessert! Like many retailers, the restaurant business uses high-margin cross-sells as a staple to maximize the Total Customer Sale Value (TCSV). Just think about the number of cross-sells you experience as you go about your day, from the recommendation of lottery tickets when you purchase gas to "other customers also bought" recommendations at the bottom of the Amazon order page.

Although retailers might be good at consistently presenting cross-sell options, those who sell business-to-business sometimes follow different models. In my experience, cross-sells in business-to-business are not as common for three reasons:

1. Few cross-sell options are available (e.g., a company selling capital equipment might have to upsell opportunities for better models or features but fails to introduce or share information about complementary cross-sell products or services).
2. The sales team needs to be more skilled and knowledgeable in presenting cross-sell options (i.e., content with making the initial sale;

 DOI: 10.4324/9781003463962-9

it's common for sales professionals to avoid delivering additional cross-selling options to their customers for fear of losing the sale).

3. Cross-sell options are considered the sole responsibility of the sales team to sell (i.e., other departments that interact with the prospect or customer, such as customer service, engineering, or operations, aren't aware of what cross-sell opportunities exist and fail to identify, share, or even involve sales when the opportunity presents itself).

If you need to capitalize on full cross-sells today and fall into any of these three categories, then read on. Alternatively, if you do have cross-sell options for your customers, you should also continue reading because, as mentioned in point 3 above, there's a good chance that your cross-sell options aren't being presented to your customers or clients as frequently or effectively as they could (which we'll also address).

INCREASE TOTAL CUSTOMER SALE VALUE

To begin with, let's be clear on precisely what a cross-sell is and isn't. The best cross-sells are products or services that you can sell to existing customers and are "complementary" to your other products or services. It's the word *complimentary* that can sometimes trip people up.

If you want to increase cross-sells, you need to identify options that complement your core and upsell offer. This is crucial because prospects and customers expect to find what they will find when they interact with your company. If the cross-sells offered do not complement your other offerings, they can create confusion for the customer and impact trust. Let me give you an example.

While driving home from the airport recently, I stopped at a red light in a small town. As I glanced to the left, I saw a storefront, and the sign-out front displayed the store's name in big, bold letters. The name was "The Product Broker." Not the clearest of names (which we will dive into at another time); however, as I glanced in the window, I noticed a wide variety of products on display for sale, mostly in bulk and of a wide variety. I concluded that this was either a consignment store or a store that sold bulk discounted items.

It was not the best choice for a business name, as it didn't tell me much without peering in the window (and I'm still unsure, trying to figure out if my guess is correct). However, then it got much worse. As my eyes returned to the sign name, I noticed a small print in the bottom right-hand corner that read "Book Your Personal Training Sessions Here."

Wait, what?

I reread the sign and suddenly had all sorts of questions. Was the owner someone who did personal training on the side? Did they have people walking in off the street who were looking to buy discounted items and were also interested in personal training? Would I trust the skills of a personal trainer who also operated a discount retail store?

See what I mean? Clarity is vital if you want to entice your customer to buy.

When your cross-sell options presented to your customer are unclear or don't align with what your customer expects of your business or your product or service offerings, they can cause confusion and even diminish trust. Neither of these are good if your goal is to make a sale. As the old saying goes, "a confused customer doesn't buy."

Here, then, are a series of steps you can take to ensure your cross-sells are clear and complimentary to your core offers and upsells:

SHAWN'S SIX RULES FOR COMPLIMENTARY CROSS-SELLS

1. There should be at least one cross-sell option for each core product(s) or service(s).
2. Cross-sell options should complement existing core product(s) or service(s).
3. All customer-facing employees should understand what cross-sell options exist for your customers.
4. Methods to introduce cross-sells should be adopted by all customer-facing employees.
5. Your sales team should understand presentation methods for cross-sells.
6. Compensation should be enticing for cross-sells introduced and sold.

Here's an example of a complimentary cross-sell (one that will appeal to your customers or clients) versus a confusing cross-sell (one that won't).

Suppose you are a dentist who offers general dentistry. Your goal is to capture more revenue from your customers (increase your share of the wallet), so you decide to bring in someone specializing in root canals. Is this a complimentary upsell option? Yes. Is it likely appealing to your customers? To some but not to the majority. Not everyone sitting in your chair will likely need a root canal.

In this case, a complimentary upsell is something that most dentists' clients could benefit from and have a need for. So, offering a service such as teeth whitening would be a better option, as nearly every patient, regardless of age, could use and want teeth whitening. If your dentistry only served clients aged 50+ in a region where several large employers offered dental insurance, root canals are a complimentary cross-sell option.

WHY YOU DON'T CLOSE MORE CROSS-SELLS

Over the years, I've observed several reasons why cross-sells are either non-existent or exist but are simply not being sold. The most common reason is often a lack of cross-sell options that complement existing products or services. It's difficult to sell cross-sells when there aren't any that appeal to the customer.

Next to a lack of complimentary cross-sells, skills (or a lack thereof) are the second most common reason companies don't consistently sell their cross-sell offers. This skills gap is most often a result of sales (and other customer-facing roles) needing to be made aware of how and when to present and close cross-sells with customers.

Lastly, a lack of cross-sells closed can be the result of a limiting belief that sales, customer service, or even company executives hold. The belief is that cross-sells, although available, are simply not appealing to the customer or client, and as a result presenting such cross-sells threatens the main (or original) sale. In other words, customers will decide when to invest in a cross-sell. Not only is this a dangerous belief to hold, but it's also completely ridiculous.

Fortunately, resolving these issues is simple and manageable. Let's start with the most obvious: identifying cross-sells that appeal to your ideal customers.

SHAWN'S CROSS-SELL IDENTIFICATION METHOD

1. Identify the key sectors you sell products or services to.
2. Identify the challenges your existing products or services address or resolve (by sector).
3. Identify the gaps or challenges your ideal customers must purchase other products or services to address that complement your existing products or services.
4. From these gaps, develop a list of cross-sell options that would further enhance the value your customers receive from you if you could resolve these issues.
5. Field test these cross-sell options by discussing with existing customers or clients.
6. Finalize your list of cross-sell options.

If, after applying this exercise, you have identified several complimentary cross-sells, you'll need to address any possible limiting beliefs before you train your team on how to introduce and close these cross-sells.

Cross-sells seem more complex than upsells, which are simply an improved or premium version of your main product or service. For example, I'm not offering you more of what you want but something different that compliments what you seek to buy. In my work with sales teams and their organizations, increasing cross-sell opportunities, we often address this issue by addressing several false, usually limiting beliefs. Take a moment to review this list, and ask yourself, "Do these false beliefs impact my team's ability (or my ability) to cross-sell?

False Belief #1: Cross-sells must be of lower value to be appealing.
False Belief #2: Cross-sells should only be presented by sales.
False Belief #3: There is a limited window to present cross-sells.
False Belief #4: You can only have one cross-sell option for each sale.

Let's discuss overcoming these limiting beliefs and broaden your perspective on how and when you can (and should) present cross-sell options.

False Belief #1: Cross-sells must be of lower value than the primary product. A cross-sell can be any value you choose and is not constrained by the value of the initial product you are presenting.

Following our earlier example of dentists, after having some gum surgery at a specialty dentist's office (who only focused on doing specialized work), they recommended new veneers on my front teeth, which were far more expensive than any work they had done to date. I've worked with a mining equipment manufacturer who cross-sells additional specialized equipment that can be ordered as attachments to their equipment, and due to the complexity of these attachments, many are equal or higher in cost to the original equipment sold.

False Belief #2: Only sales can present cross-sell options. Building on our earlier discussion, departments outside of sales are often involved before, during, and post-sale with the customer. These include engineering, operations, marketing, and others. If these departments know the cross-sell options, they can make suggestions or recommendations where appropriate, like sales. Also, like sales, if there are better parties to speak to specific technical aspects of the cross-sell options, they can make introductions to other parties who can. Referring to my earlier example of my client who sold mining equipment, we equipped their engineers, who often engaged with potential customers early in the sales process, with the information, language, and confidence to mention cross-sell options when appropriate. If the customer were interested, they would bring sales back into the discussion.

False Belief #3: There is a limited window of opportunity to present cross-sells. This is not true. Unless you oppose revising or updating your sale agreement, you can recommend cross-selling options at any point during the customer relationship. Timing might be the only barrier here to address. For example, regarding the mining equipment manufacturer, as I mentioned above, cross-selling an attachment after the unit has been built often requires retrofits. As a result, many of the sales and engineering teams hesitated to recommend cross-sells after initiating the build. To overcome this perceived barrier, we ensured retrofits were possible and then trained the employees to present cross-sells after the build had commenced.

False Belief #4: You can only have one cross-sell per sale. Often, the limitation here is needing more cross-sell options or employees not being clear on the complimentary cross-sell options that exist and, as a result, believing there are few, if any, cross-sell options. By mapping cross-sell options against primary sale options, you can easily equip all employees with the information and confidence needed to recommend multiple cross-sells. In an insurance brokerage, account managers only offered cross-sell options when customers asked about additional options. They often provided one cross-sell for fear of confusing the customer. We mapped out various cross-sell options based on typical customer questions. We turned this into a marketing document that the account managers can speak to and share with customers to clarify their options further.

With these limiting beliefs now addressed, let's move on to discuss how you can increase your cross-sell opportunities and multiply your sales.

HOW A STRONG UPSELL SECURES A CROSS-SELL

By this point, I'm hopeful you've realized that for every sale you make, there are significant opportunities to increase the size (and value) of that sale IF you have upsell options that satisfy the additional needs of your prospect and exist with COMPLIMENTARY cross-sells. The key to capitalizing on upsell and cross-sell opportunities is considering who should be involved and who is skilled to share these options with customers. Like our previous discussions, when you equip other employees who are directly and indirectly communicating and interacting with your prospects and customers with the exact skills, language, and confidence to mention upsells and cross-sells, you will significantly increase your ability to close these new selling opportunities.

But there is more to making cross-sells than just mentioning them during conversations. This is where your Sales Multiplier Formula comes into play. It informs how and when you and anyone you engage to support your cross-sells mention them. What you'll notice as we expand the framework is that your cross-sells are best presented after your initial upsell attempt. In other words, when you position the initial upsell correctly, you increase your chances of making a cross-sell.

There are several reasons why a good upsell, which is complimentary to the core product or service and presented by the right person at the appropriate time, will help you close a cross-sell.

To begin with, consider that a recent study by ignite80[1] found that several factors influence B2B customers' buying interactions, namely:

1. Customers prefer interactions that offer choice over a single solution.
2. Customers prefer human connection to assist with making their buying choices.
3. Customers prefer being involved in resolving their problems or challenges versus a quick fix.

So, when you offer your customers or clients a choice rather than a single solution and help them explore the benefits of that choice, you influence the buying decision.

In addition to these psychological influences, there is another reason why positioning a strong upsell will increase your chances of a cross-sell. *Your prospect or customer is already ready to buy, and complimentary upsell options, which add further value for your prospect, directly influence their willingness to increase their investment to achieve the additional value.* In other words, if you are about to close a deal or have just recently closed an agreement, your customer is in what I refer to as The Close Zone and, therefore, is comfortable with handing over their money in exchange for your product or service. Their wallets, or budgets, are open and available. Figure 7.1 describes how the close zone works.

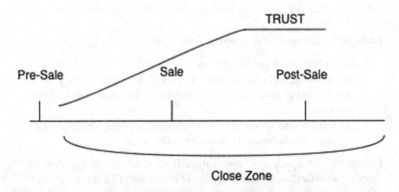

FIGURE 7.1
The Close Zone pre-during-post buy (specific time), comfort level with you, budget available, trust in handing over to your company

This book and the Sales Multiplier Formula are designed to entice you to think big. They provide you with a proven method for introducing multiple additional sales opportunities to every prospect and customer your team interacts with. When you apply the formula, offering a good upsell option paired with a complimentary cross-sell will significantly increase your chances of multiplying every sale and increasing your customer sale value.

Let's look at examples of a good upsell, which, when paired with a complimentary cross-sell, would increase your chances of closing both.

Example 1: Manufacturer of Widgets Example:

Core Product: Steel components (i.e., brackets)
Upsell Options: Increased Volume, Different (Premium) Materials, Increased Quality Assurance
Cross-Sell Options: Custom Engineering Services, Bolts for Bracket Installation, Shipping

An example of an upsell offer that entices a cross-sell is offering the customer increased quality assurance checks (for tighter tolerances) and engineering design services (to minimize the costs of achieving the tighter tolerances).

Example 2: Commercial Insurance Example:

Core Product: Commercial insurance policies
Upsell Options: Reduced Deductible, Increased Coverage, Customized insurance options
Cross-Sell Options: Financial Investment Services, Employee Benefit Services, Retirement Planning Services

An example of an upsell offer that entices a cross-sell is offering additional insurance options for post-employment (i.e., after an employee retires) coupled with Retirement Planning Services to help employees transition into retirement.

Example 3: Managed Services Provider Example:

Core Product: Managed IT Services
Upsell Options: Increased Service Coverage, Premium Service Levels (i.e., onsite support, reduced response times), Program Customization Options
Cross-Sell Options: Customized IT Consulting Services, Complimentary Hardware or Software, IT Recruitment Services

Example of an upsell offer that entices a cross-sell is offering Program Customization Options in conjunction with Customized IT Consulting (to identify the best options for the client).

Example 4: Commercial Land Surveying Company Example:

Core Product: Traditional Land Surveying Services
Upsell Options: Construction Surveys, Topographic Surveys, Elevation
    Certificates
Cross-Sell Options: Geomatic Services, Construction Design Services,
    Residential Survey Services

An example of an upsell offer that entices a cross-sell is offering construction surveys coupled with construction design services (that incorporate the survey results).

Example 5: Recruitment Firm Example:

Core Product: Recruitment Services
Upsell Options: Increase Roles to Fill, Long-term Contract, Job
    Description Development
Cross-Sell Options: Employee Benefits Services, Human Resource
    Information Software, Employee Onboarding Consulting Services

An example of an upsell offer that entices a cross-sell is offering a long-term recruitment contract (i.e., one year for all recruitment) coupled with Employee Onboard Consulting Services (to retain new hires).

Positioning a complimentary upsell that your prospect has a potential need for and that adds value is foundational to providing a cross-sell offer that only makes sense for your customer to invest in. Additionally, you'll notice that every good cross-sell must achieve three main goals:

1. It must complement the main product or service you already sell.
2. It must address the broader challenge(s) or objective(s) your customer or client has.
3. Combining your core product, upsell, and cross-sell must increase the overall value your prospect or customer receives from investing in your company.

Now that we've identified how to present your best upsell and bundle it to entice closing a cross-sell, let's discuss *when to introduce cross-sell options* to increase the chances of your prospect or customer investing in them.

SELECTING THE BEST TIME TO PRESENT YOUR CROSS-SELL

The key to any good cross-selling is to introduce the idea of cross-selling to your prospects before they buy. Let that sink in for a moment. Upsell options are often a "better version" of what your customer or client is already considering. In contrast, the cross-sell is unique and designed to add value and differentiate your offer in the market. It can be more of a stretch from the initial sale than an upsell, and as a result, you need to begin planting seeds on the cross-sell early.

Suppose you visit a restaurant for dinner, and while ordering a hamburger, you want the 6oz burger patty or the 4oz patty. If the price difference is reasonable, and supposing you are hungry, you'll accept the upsell and ask for the 6oz version of the burger. This is a typical example of an upsell for restaurants, but what about a cross-sell?

A common cross-sell that most restaurants offer is dessert. Typically, the server suggests dessert *after the main course is complete.* This is NOT a suitable method of introducing the cross-sell because, using our example above, there is a chance the customer has already filled up on the 6oz hamburger (upsell) and, therefore, doesn't have any room left for the cross-sell (dessert). The best restaurant servers mention the dessert at the very beginning, often after they introduce themselves and identify the "features" from the menu. They present this using language such as "You'll want to make sure you save room for dessert because tonight we have our special (you fill in your favorite dessert here)."

Suppose I am positioning my cross-sell for success. In that case, I must mention it early in my discussions with prospects, often during the discovery dialogue (in our restaurant example, this would be while the customer reviews the menu).

Let's look at how you can position the cross-sell earlier, referring to the examples we discussed earlier.

Example 1: Language to Position a Cross-Sell for a Manufacturer of Steel Components:

"Some of our best customers use our Engineering services to help design their brackets and ensure the best fit, form, and function while maintaining the lowest cost and highest tolerances."

Example 2: Language to Position a Cross-Sell for a Commercial Insurer:

"Many of our clients also use our retirement planning services to ensure their employees select the best possible insurance and investment options."

Example 3: Managed Services Provider Example:

"We often recommend that our clients consider cybersecurity as part of our work together. It's the best way to ensure that our services support your strategic goals."

Example 4: Commercial Land Surveying Company Example:

"Unlike many of our competitors, we also offer Construction Design Services, which minimize your need to engage several different service providers and ensure you gain maximum benefits from the survey work we do."

Example 5: Recruitment Firm Example:

"Our best clients have found that our Employee Onboarding solutions ensure the hires they invest in are retained over the long term."

You'll notice in these examples that it's very easy to mention cross-sell options in the early part of discussions with prospects and that doing so makes it much easier to position the cross-sell as a necessary investment if the prospect wants to gain the most value from working with your company. I call this "planting cross-sell seeds," and doing so is the best method of ensuring your cross-sell is desirable by your customers or clients.

Considering this, the steps to introducing a cross-sell then are as follows:

SHAWN'S STEPS TO INTRODUCING A SUCCESSFUL CROSS-SELL

1. Mention cross-sell options during initial prospect discovery dialogues.
2. Reinforce the value of (relevant) cross-sell options at the pre-proposal stage.
3. Introduce relevant cross-sell options in your proposal or quote.
4. Reference cross-sells (from the proposal) while closing the sale.
5. Post-sale: reference any cross-sells not invested in that remain relevant.
6. Post-sale: include cross-selling options in Account Management or Follow-up activities.

As discussed earlier in this book, cross-selling is broader than just the sales department. Any role that interacts with the customer can mention cross-sell options, and the more consistent the messaging and frequency, the greater the likelihood that the prospect or customer will invest in the cross-sell.

Let's look at some examples of who you might involve in the abovementioned steps.

Step 1: Sales, Engineering
Step 2: Sales, Engineering, Estimators
Step 3: Sales, Engineering, Estimators
Step 4: Sales, Customer Service
Step 5: Sales, Customer Service, Account Management, Project Management, Operations, Production, Shipping
Step 6: Sales, Customer Service, Account Management, Project Management, Operations, Production, Shipping

The key to success with cross-selling is beyond having complimentary cross-sells. A practical method (and skills) for introducing them is ensuring everyone who interacts with the customer understands the customer's business, needs, objectives, and, most importantly, what cross-sells have been suggested or recommended in early discussions (i.e., discovery dialogue). The simplest way to achieve this is to ensure all customer notes and proposals or quotes are easily accessible and shared with all relevant departments and individuals across the company. To share, you can do this the old-fashioned way by having sales prepare (and periodically update) a customer or client brief that gets circulated to all relevant parties, keeping them informed on discussions. A better way is to use your CRM software, reinforcing the need for everyone to stay current on ongoing conversations by accessing customer notes and next steps.

THE CROSS-SELL VALUE EQUATION

Fundamentally, every good cross-sell must add value to your customer or client. Being clear on the value that your cross-sell options offer new or existing customers or clients is the key to enticing and influencing them and any other departments involved in helping you position the cross-sell.

I've found in working with sales teams worldwide that most salespeople, once a sale seems evident, count themselves as lucky, and as a result, they tend not to want to "push their luck" for fear of losing the sale. This is the wrong mindset, so to overcome this, you need to suggest how your prospects receive value from the cross-sells you offer. Let's continue using the wide variety of earlier examples to demonstrate what the potential value might look like in each situation.

Example 1: Value of Engineering Design Service Cross-Sell for a Manufacturer:

Save Time: Fewer vendors or suppliers to interact with.
Improved Quality: Better integration of widgets with other products.

Example 2: Value of Retirement Planning Service Cross-Sell for an Insurance Company:

Improved Culture: Happier employees.
Increased Efficiency: Reduce reliance on Human Resources to assist individual retirees.

Example 3: Value of Cyber Security Service Cross-Sell for a Managed Services Provider:

Increased Network Uptime: Reduced risk of cybersecurity issues.
Ease of Network Management: Only one call to make to address all network-related issues.

Example 4: Value of Construction Design Service Cross-Sell for a Commercial Land Surveying Company:

Achieve Project Deadlines: Seamless transition from survey to design.
Reduced Construction Errors: Reduced construction errors due to accurate survey interpretation during construction design.

Example 5: Value of Employee Onboarding Service Cross-Sell for a Recruitment Firm:

Increased Employee Retention: Proven onboarding solutions that retain employees.
Ease of Employee Onboarding: A single source for all hiring and onboarding needs.

Make sure to include an understanding of how your cross-sells add value to chance! Be explicit in specifying the value your cross-sells provide your customers or clients and ensure everyone within your organization recognizes this.

To this point, we've broken down the upsell and the cross-sell, but what if you've mastered these and wonder what's next to multiply your sales? Well, it's time to fuel your sales opportunities by developing a lead-generation machine like no other. For more details, let's jump to the next chapter. See you there!

Sales Multiplier Mindset: A strong upsell, paired with a complimentary cross-sell, increases your chances of closing both sales and increasing your total customer sales value.

NOTE

1 https://hbr.org/2023/03/what-do-your-b2b-customers-really-want

8

Best: Generating Unstoppable Referrals

According to a study conducted by the Brevet group,[1] 91% of customers say they'd give referrals. However, only 11% of sales professionals ask for a referral. Let that sink in for a minute. In other words, most of your customers, or at least those who have had a positive experience working with your company, would be willing to provide a referral, yet they need to be asked. That's leaving money on the table 89% of the time, and that's not the way to multiply your sales.

To begin with, we're faced with the obvious question – why aren't customers being asked for a referral? Is there a misguided belief that the experience your customers or clients received is not worthy of a referral? After an initial bad experience, you may have forgotten how to best ask for a referral or that you should ask at all. Either of these is possible, but in my experience, the problem runs much more profound.

Let's start by explaining why you don't get referrals today. In my experience, most sales professionals *have asked for a referral*, often very early in their career or during the early days of working with their current company, when they had little experience. Being new to sales or your company and its products or services, they asked in a very vague manner, which, if they were fortunate, led to a vague answer. Most likely, you've received a "let me think about it" response, and then, presuming the customer or client would circle back if they did think of someone to refer, you moved on.

For example, they may have asked, "Susan, do you know anyone who might be interested in purchasing our insurance?" The answer they received from Susan at the time was either a flat no or a "let me think

DOI: 10.4324/9781003463962-10

about it." It's possible after this experience that they asked someone else, possibly even attempted to obtain a referral on a few more occasions, only to be continuously told "no" or "let me think about it," after hearing which they eventually gave up, convinced that referrals aren't easily obtained, and instead deciding to wait for their customers or clients to offer up referrals.

Besides, a happy customer will automatically offer up a referral, won't they? Well, if you refer to the statistics at the beginning of this chapter, in most instances they won't.

Obtaining referrals, like any other sales methodology, requires a combination of applying the correct method at the right time to be successful. You may believe your method or timing could be better to obtain a referral, and in my experience, you're likely right. This step, however, is so crucial to your sales multiplier formula that I'd suggest if you do nothing else as a result of reading this book, you introduce the referral method I'm about to share with you. So pay attention!

MASTER THIS AND EXPLODE YOUR SALES TO NEW LEVELS

An adequately designed referral system, monitored, and adjusted for ongoing impact, can single-handedly multiply your sales exponentially. Referrals are genuinely your secret sales weapon if you want to multiply your sales, and the good news (as demonstrated in the above study) is that your customers and clients expect to be asked for a referral! Not only do they expect to be asked, but they expect this to happen on multiple occasions during the sales process. So, do you think you could improve upon your current referral system? (Hint: The answer is yes!)

Let's dive into why most referrals lead to a "let me think about it" response. There are right and wrong ways to ask for a referral. In my earlier example, I was asking a vague question: "Do you know someone..." Vague questions result in vague answers. The truth is, every single prospect and customer you've ever interacted with knows someone you could sell to. They know many people, but without any specificity in describing who you can help, any request you make falls flat.

Think back to when you were in school (possibly you're still in school). Do your teachers ask vague questions on your tests, or do they ask you specific questions that elicit a specific answer? It's most often the latter of the two.

If you want to obtain a referral, then you need to ask a specific question. Here's an example of a more specific question I could have asked my client: "Do you know your neighbor Valerie? I'm wondering if she might like me to cut her lawn." Then, presuming she did know Valerie, I would have followed up by asking, "Would you be willing to make an introduction?"

Do you see the difference between my original referral request and this more specific one? Even if my client didn't know Valerie, there's a chance she'll mention someone else who might appreciate having their lawn cut now that I've asked her a specific question. Specificity is critical if you want a referral.

Now, if you've been specific about "who" you are seeking in your referral request, then there may be a different issue at play. Think about a product or service you use on a regular basis that you're very happy with. It could be where you get your hair cut or a comfortable pair of shoes you repeatedly buy. You may visit a chiropractor regularly who has helped to keep you walking upright. Whatever product or service you are pleased with, take a moment to write a list of these products or services on a piece of paper or take notes on your phone.

Next, consider the last time you purposefully introduced someone to this favorite company, product, or service. I don't mean that you mentioned it when they complained about getting a bad haircut or having a sore back, but rather, you proactively took time out of your schedule to reach out to your network and offer to introduce them to these companies, their products, or services. For example, you reached out to a colleague or friend and introduced them to your chiropractor via an email, or you took them physically to the store where you purchased your shoes for no reason other than out of the goodness of your heart. My guess is that although you mentioned your great experience with these products or services, you likely did not go out of your way to make an immediate and purposeful introduction or connection to them.

Herein lies the second problem. A referral often requires that our customers or clients *do something*. It requires their most important resource, their time. Because time is a priority, most people tend to only spend time on giving referrals if there is a direct and immediately valuable return on their time invested.

Let's return to my earlier statement that most sales professionals have requested a referral but have yet to receive one. In most instances, it's because they didn't make it easy for their customer or client, and they positioned the referral request as something that required their prospect's time to complete, without offering sufficient value in return. They might have asked, but they needed to make it easier for the customer to make the introduction. The result? Well, if the ask was done well, then their client or customer might be thinking about the amount of time and effort required to make an introduction, and as a result, their response is, "Let me think about it." If the referral is expected to require any effort on your customer's behalf, you can expect this to be their answer.

So, in addition to being specific about who you are seeking, it's also essential to give your prospect something to get a referral in return. The value exchange convinces your customer of the benefit of investing their time in your referral.

Aside from these gaps in your referral process, there are several other reasons why you may not be receiving a referral. Even an ecstatic customer or client, faced with a specific request for a referral that isn't overly demanding of their time, may decide not to move forward for any of the following additional reasons:

1. They are busy, and referring others is a low priority.
2. They aren't immediately clear on who they could introduce us to.
3. They must figure out what to say if they introduce us.
4. They need to figure out when the right time is to make an introduction.
5. They need to see an immediate personal benefit to making the introduction.

When you realize the many obstacles that keep your customers or clients from offering referrals, it's easy to understand why you aren't repeatedly obtaining referrals. The question then shifts from "why" I am not receiving referrals to "how" I can obtain referrals given these various obstacles. What are the steps to ensure that all my satisfied customers or clients are eager and willing to make introductions to others?

You'll need to put eight steps into practice, which form the foundation of your sales multiplier referral system.

SHAWN'S EIGHT RULES FOR UNSTOPPABLE REFERRALS

1. You mention the desire for a referral during the discovery dialogue with every prospect.
2. Ideal referral candidates are clearly defined (i.e., type of company, title, position).
3. Referral asks are pre-determined and planned for each customer or client's journey.
4. Measures are in place to track when referral asks take place.
5. A referral request is made for every lost sale (pending the relationship remains intact).
6. Every lost customer or client is asked for a referral (pending a solid relationship).
7. Existing customers or clients are asked for a referral every six months at a minimum.
8. Other customer or client-facing employees are skilled and confident in helping you solicit referrals (more on this in a moment!).

It's easy to see how adding these steps significantly increases your chance of obtaining referrals. I recognize that these steps might seem a bit overwhelming or possibly too difficult to introduce all at once. If this is the case for you, then just start by addressing the two foundational components mentioned earlier.

First, when a referral is requested, be specific in your request. Who do you want to connect with, and how can your customer or client best do this?

Second, ensure that the ask isn't a burden for your client or customer but rather makes it easy for them to say yes. For example, you can suggest that you reach out (with your customer's permission) and mention your client's suggestion that you call. You could also ask if there is someone they'd like to invite to an upcoming lunch or an event you might be having with your client.

Aside from these steps, the next most crucial step that will add rocket fuel to your referrals is expanding the ability to ask for referrals beyond yourself. What does this mean? Let's dive in and discuss this often controversial, yet essential component of your Sales Multiplier Formula next.

YOU ARE MISSING REFERRAL OPPORTUNITIES (HERE'S WHY)

In most selling situations, sales only involve finding and building relationships with the customer or client. Once the sale is made, they often turn over the relationship to others within their company. If you think about it, your customer or client spends most of the time with your company, its products, or services AFTER they interact with sales. Figure 8.1 demonstrates this timeline.

Because of this, if you want to increase the number of referrals you earn from your customers or clients, you need to broaden your perspective on not only who to ask, when to ask, and how to ask. You must also

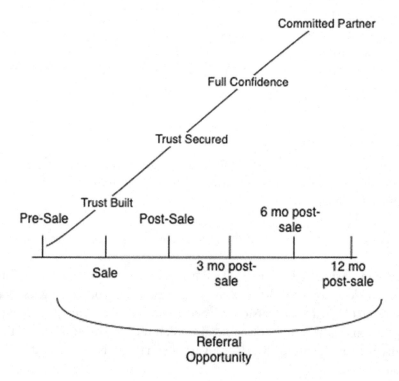

FIGURE 8.1

Timeline for prospect referral opportunities

extend your reach by considering who can make the request. For example, jumping back into a relationship that has been transitioned to Inside Sales to solicit a referral 6 months after the sale is complete might be awkward for you and your customer or client. Start by thinking about who your customer or client might feel most comfortable making a referral to. In other words, when the referral request is made, who has been the most involved with the customer leading up to this point? If you sell a product versus a service, the answer to this question can differ, as seen in the example below:

Product Sale Involvement:

Initial sale: Involvement includes Sales, Engineering, Design
Post-sale (3 months): Involvement includes Customer Service, Production, Operations
Post-sale (6 months): Involvement includes Customer Service, Shipping

Service Sale Involvement:

Initial sale: Involvement includes Sales, Service Design
Post-sale (3 months): Involvement includes Customer Onboarding, Account Management
Post-sale (6 months): Involvement includes Account Management

These are simply examples of who is typically involved with your customers or clients, and depending on what you sell, may differ for your company. For this reason, take a few minutes to map out who specifically in your company interacts with your customers pre-sale and then at various points post-sale. This list identifies who can request the referral at different stages in your customer or client's journey.

Next, it's important to discuss how pre- and post-sale referrals differ. Your customer or client's relationship with your company and your products or services differ depending on where they are in their buying journey. The relationship changes because of shifting expectations that exist as the relationship evolves. Figure 8.2 demonstrates how expectations shift.

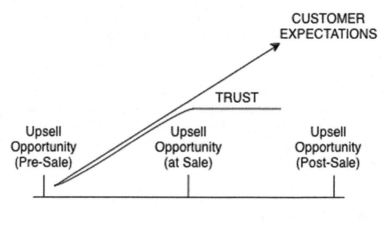

Customer Sale Journey

FIGURE 8.2

Changes in customer expectations post sale

In a pre-sale referral, the ability to obtain a referral (or referrals) is based on the preconceived notions of:

Your company and its reputation in the market.
The perceived quality of your products or services.
Initial interactions with your employees.

Obtaining a pre-sale referral comes when *you incentivize your customer or client to provide the referral* since they have yet to have a strong relationship with your company or its product or service. For example, you might offer a bonus, a discount on the pending sale, or future sales.

In a post-sale referral, the ability to obtain a referral (or ongoing referrals) is based on different factors such as:

The experience a customer or client has with your company.
Interactions with your companies' employees.
The ability of your product or service to satisfy their needs.

Obtaining a post-sale referral comes when you capitalize on *positive points in your customer or client relationship*. It would help to design a customer journey with specific points at which your employees will solicit referrals. This might include points during your product or service delivery, a post-sale follow-up call, an onsite product installation, and so on.

YOUR SALES MULTIPLIER REFERRAL STRATEGY AND TOOLKIT

Earlier, I discussed that most sales professionals have asked for a referral at one point or another; however, they haven't ended up obtaining the desired referral because they are not specific enough in their ask. As a result, not receiving a referral or being promised that the customer or client would "think about it," but receiving nothing has turned most sales professionals away from asking for referrals. The missing piece is having a referral process that can be executed and achieves the desired results (in our case, it is a steady stream of solicited and unsolicited referrals).

Let's take the idea of a referral strategy one step further. The name of this book is Sales Multiplier, and I couldn't, in good faith, provide you with a typical referral strategy and expect you to be content. So, we will amplify your referral process to engage others and generate an unstoppable stream of referrals.

Let's begin by building on our earlier discussions and walking through the steps necessary to develop your Sales Multiplier Referral Process. You can do this using a piece of paper, a Word document, or a template I've developed for you at salesmultiplierbook.com

Steps to Developing Your Sales Multiplier Referral Process

As mentioned above, to ensure your Sales Multiplier Referral Process works, you'll need to engage other departments to support you. If you are a sales executive or president in your company, engaging other departments to support your strategy is likely not that challenging. However, if you are in middle management or you're a sales professional, then your approach must be different.

In the former instance, work through the steps below or have someone leading your sales teamwork through these steps. Then, they will share with you the resulting process for your review, approval, and rollout to the other departments involved.

Suppose you are in middle management or sales, and you don't have authority over the other impacted departments. In that case, I'd like you to develop the process using the steps below, then take it to your manager, vice president, or direct to the company president if you have a strong relationship, and discuss your objectives in introducing the strategy (to generate consistent, repeat referrals), and why you'll need to involve others in the strategy (as the relationship with your clients or customers tend to transfer to different departments or people throughout their journey). Getting the support at an executive level will be necessary if you want the Sales Multiplier Referral Strategy to work as it should.

Step 1: Define your ideal company or clients to work with. Include details such as sector, type of company (i.e., publicly owned or privately held), location, and size of company.

Step 2: Identify who within your ideal company or clients is your target prospect. Include details such as title(s), specific pain points or needs, and best methods to reach them (i.e., telephone, email, social). Note: Your target prospect must have the decision-making authority to approve investment in what you sell!

Step 3: Identify who within your ideal company or clients influences your target prospect's decisions. These might include others who work for your target but are regularly called upon for their input on decisions and who can influence your target prospect's decisions (e.g., Engineering or Operations).

Step 4: Identify several scripts that can be used to ask for a referral. These are specific statements that you or others can use to describe the type of company and who within those companies you'd like to be introduced to. Use the information captured thus far to inform these scripts.

Step 5: Identify who within your company interacts directly with your existing customers or clients. This can include everyone from reception to customer service to accounts receivable. If there are multiple people within each department who might interact with your customer or client (e.g., your client may interact with one of many customer service representatives), then simply define the department rather than the person.

Step 6: Identify your customer or client's journey from the initial point of contact to becoming an ongoing customer or client. These might include stages such as Initial Meeting, Presentation, Proposal, Close, Onboarding, and Initial Shipment. Ensure that your stages progress throughout the lifetime of a customer or client, meaning that once a new client has been onboarded, you should set regular intervals for asking for referrals. I'd recommend it at least once every six months.

Step 7: Identify the departments or people that interact (or may interact) with the customer or client for each journey stage. This may be a single department or multiple. The goal is that for each stage you've identified, at least one person or department interacts with the customer at this stage.

Step 8: Develop a method to track customer referral asks for each stage of their journey. This is best done using a good CRM software; however, since you will need to provide many people access, it may be easier or more cost-effective to use a Google Doc or Excel sheet. If you go this route, create several columns and label them as a step in the customer or client journey (from step 6 above). The goal is to have the individual who interacts check the box when they ask for the referral, allowing you to ensure all possible referral request opportunities have been capitalized on.

Step 9: Introduce your referral strategy (thus far) to all the individuals or departments you identified in step 7. Your goal here is to educate them on the referral opportunities and share several referral scripts that they might use. Additionally, you'll need to demonstrate the tracking system you've developed to ensure they have full access and the ability to update the applicable stages once they ask.

Step 10: Trial run your referral strategy by selecting customers or clients at various stages in their journey. For example, you might choose a prospect, a new customer or client, and a long-term customer or client. Then, have the appropriate department or individual use the scripts you developed earlier to request the referral. Once you've done a dry run, bring the individuals involved to discuss what needs to be improved (e.g., better scripts) and how you can make these improvements to generate more referrals.

There you have it. Ten steps to introduce and launch your Sales Multiplier Referral Process. This is the first step to getting your referral system off the ground, but to experience success quickly, you'll need a few additional resources. Let's discuss those next.

If you'd like a template to work through for your Sales Multiplier Referral Strategy, visit salesmultiplierbook.com.

Now let's look at some tools and resources to support your referral strategy.

Every prospect, client, or customer represents an opportunity to generate a referral. A study by SaaSquatch[2] identified that every customer you have can generate 2.68 referrals on average. Let's take this study and apply a more conservative number to your business. Let's agree that for every customer or client you have today, you can generate a minimum of one high-quality referral. Further, your closing ratio is already strong, and the fact that these are referrals gives you a 100% chance of closing the deal. What happens if you double your sales by receiving and closing a referral for every customer or client you have today? How would that impact your sales? Your revenue? Your income?

For starters, it makes a strong case for focusing on developing and launching your referral strategy. However, to do so, you will need some resources in place to ensure your strategy is executed effectively (as you intend) and consistently (by everyone involved). Here is a list of the resources you need to develop to ensure your referral strategy is executed as you intend.

Shawn's Referral Strategy Resources

1. Confirm your referral stages:
   a. Identify the best times to ask a new prospect for a referral.
   b. Identify the best times to ask customers for a referral.
   c. Identify the best times to ask past customers for a referral.
2. Develop your referral regime:
   a. When will you ask for referrals weekly (what day, what time, how many)?
   b. How will you hold yourself accountable for asking for referrals?
   c. What time will you set aside to assess progress and make any improvements?
   d. Block time in your calendar for these activities.
3. Develop referral scripts:
   a. Identify each department involved in your customer or client's journey.
   b. Determine how and when they can best help you to solicit referrals.
   c. Develop a referral script for each department (how they can mention the referral).
   d. Introduce and train each department on how to use this script.

4. Referral tracking by customer or client:
   a. Determine where you will log the completion of each referral request.
   b. Launch your referral strategy and monitor each department's success rate.
   c. Provide additional training or coaching as required.
5. Referral follow-up tracking:
   a. Define your referral follow-up scripts and process them.
   b. Determine the timing for referral follow-ups and how you'll track this (it may take more than one ask to obtain the referral).
   c. Set up a system to ensure you meet these follow-up targets (i.e., set the dates in your calendar or CRM).
6. Identify your referral key performance indicators (KPIs):
   a. Develop your referral KPIs, which should include the following:
      i. The number of referral requests is required for each customer or client.
      ii. Status of each referral request (i.e., received, denied, discussed) by customer or client.
      iii. Department success rate at receiving referrals (i.e., Engineering successfully receives referrals, whereas Customer Service does not).
      iv. Referral script success rate (which scripts have the greatest success at winning referrals).

Depending on the complexity of your product or service, you may want to include other KPIs. For example, if you typically interact with multiple different departments at each customer or client, you may want to track the success of receiving referrals from these different departments.

Visit www.salesmultiplierbook.com for a copy of example scripts and other resources to launch your referral strategy and multiply your sales.

WHEN IT COMES TO REFERRALS, LESS ISN'T MORE

I intend to broaden your perspective on the referral opportunities you could generate if you introduced and successfully launched the Sales Multiplier Referral Process. Suppose you have customers or clients who are content with what you sell and the experience they receive from interacting with your company. In that case, you generate significant additional business with nothing more than an effective referral strategy.

You will notice, however, that simply leaving referral requests in the hands of sales is NOT the way to generate unstoppable referrals. Sure, some salespeople are highly effective at asking and receiving referrals. However, you need a system, one that engages a variety of customer- or client-facing roles, to generate the referrals that are waiting for you to capitalize on.

In other words, generating referrals consistently and predictably requires five key ingredients:

1. You must accept that referrals can come at any stage of your customer or client journey with your company.
2. You need to engage everyone who is customer- or client-facing to accept their responsibility for generating referrals.
3. You need a robust Referral Process that defines how you will generate referrals.
4. You must develop and introduce scripts, measures, and training to ensure the strategy is executed effectively.
5. You should continuously monitor and revisit what is working and what isn't, allowing you to make necessary adjustments or updates to your unstoppable referral machine.

Now that you have your referral strategy, let's discuss building a culture that supports your new (and effective) sales measures. Jump over to Chapter 9, and I'll see you there!

Sales Multiplier Mindset: When you ask someone for a referral, you are asking for their most valuable resource – their time. Ensure that you practice a "give to get" approach to soliciting referrals.

NOTES

1 https://blog.thebrevetgroup.com/21-mind-blowing-sales-stats
2 https://www.saasquatch.com/blog/rs-17-referral-marketing-statistics/

Part 3

Building Momentum with Your Sales Multiplier Formula

With your sales multiplier formula now in place, your goal should be to increase the momentum and speed of new sales as a result. The next several chapters will walk you through how you can increase momentum, the steps to take, and critical areas of your formula to monitor to ensure you remain on track.

Chapter 9 is for sales leaders and executives who have the desire and ability to engage the broader organization and build a sales culture. Chapters 10 through 12 discuss specific implementation strategies, key measures to monitor progress, and methods to use your formula and continue to attract new customers.

DOI: 10.4324/9781003463962-11

9

The Foundation: Build a Sales-Centric Culture

As you can tell from the earlier discussions in this book, building a culture focused on sales can only multiply your sales. Sales professionals can influence it on a one-to-one relationship basis, but they often need everyone who is customer-facing on board. That's where you come in. In this chapter, we'll walk through the steps you can take to build a more sales-centric culture in your company.

Note: This chapter can still be valuable even if you are not a sales leader or executive. It will demonstrate further steps you can take to improve the buy-in and support of other departments who influence your customers or clients and, ultimately, your ability to multiply your sales.

While recently watching the movie *Ford v Ferrari*,[1] I was reminded of just how challenging influencing the behaviors of others can be. The film, released in 2019, tells the story of automotive designer Carroll Shelby and British driver Ken Miles, whom Henry Ford II and Lee Iacocca hired to build a race car to defeat Ferrari in the 1966 24 Hours of Le Mans race, which took place in France.

Lee Iacocca selects Carroll Shelby to head up their racing program to win the 24 Hours of Le Mans race in France. Shelby, a well-known racer and car designer, selects Ken Miles as his driver. Miles, portrayed as a hot-tempered race car driver, isn't well received by some of the executives at Ford, and Shelby finds himself in the awkward position of attempting to build a winning car and race team while keeping Ford executives (several of whom don't appreciate Miles's temper) at bay. The challenges Shelby faces in managing the dynamic of these relationships are clear and appear far more strenuous than building the car that ultimately won Le Mans.

DOI: 10.4324/9781003463962-12

You might not be building a winning race team or having an employee or department as hot-tempered as Ken Miles in the movie, but you will face similar challenges that Shelby faced during these critical years for Ford. So, strap in and hold on; this part of the ride will get bumpy.

HOW TO BUILD A TEAM TO SUPPORT MULTIPLYING YOUR SALES

Many years ago, I led a national not-for-profit member-based association. My role focused on growing the member base. In retrospect, this work was challenging, and we did achieve our goal of significant member growth. However, our steps to achieve growth were relatively easy and strategic. Our core focus was to ensure that every employee recognized their role's influence on our customers, directly or indirectly (or both), and we equipped them with strategies to help us grow our revenue. Underlying our methods was the Sales Multiplier Formula.

It was easy to agree with the employees about the importance of our customers to the Business. Everyone fundamentally understood this. The intricate work came when we began placing our members and their best interests at the forefront of all our initiatives, decisions, and operating methods. We struggled to balance the desire to be operationally efficient and profitable while still serving and supporting our members (customers).

Since then, I've worked with dozens of organizations, from insurance companies to banks, capital equipment manufacturers to technology companies. All use the same fundamental steps we successfully applied to achieve growth, resulting in a sales-centric culture.

In the first part of this book, we discussed the role your employees play in developing and supporting sales. By this point, if you genuinely want to multiply your sales, you recognize the opportunity to introduce the sales multiplier framework into your organization. To succeed, however, you must create a culture that appreciates and supports sales. It's not an option but rather a necessity.

Presuming you recognize and appreciate this need, let's turn our attention to what is required to transition your organization's culture from its current state (non-sales-focused) to what I call a sales-centric culture.

YOUR SALES-CENTRIC CULTURE BEGINS WITH LEADERSHIP

I've used the word "culture" here for a reason; however, let me clarify why. To begin with, I'm not going to start discussing developing your vision and values. Are these significant components of a corporate culture? Sure. But what I've learned after working with hundreds of companies over nearly two decades is that to the average employee, a company's vision and values are demonstrated by leadership across the company. Let me explain.

You could, like so many organizations, invest time and money by spending several days nestled away at a retreat formulating your vision and value statements; devote additional money to have it printed on banners and coffee mugs that you display back at your facility, but at the end of the day if the leaders in the company don't behave and speak in a manner that aligns with the vision and values, then those catchy vision phrases won't be worth the mug they're printed on. Leaders must demonstrate the company's values every day if they want to influence the culture.

For this reason, creating a more sales-centric culture begins with influencing how leaders within the company think, act, and behave. This includes how they focus their time, the language they use, and how they prioritize the activities of their departments or teams. When you realize that leadership, particularly those on the front lines of a company, determines the culture adopted and accepted, suddenly the idea of shifting or evolving company culture is manageable, or at least it should be manageable.

If you are an executive in your company, be it the President, Vice President of Sales, Director of Sales, or otherwise, your focus must be engaging everyone in recognizing the importance of sales and their influence on existing and future sales. More specifically, you'll need to emphasize the following areas:

Help employees realize their direct and indirect influences on your customers or clients. When meeting with, speaking to, or working with departments outside of sales, connect the dots between employee roles and responsibilities and customer needs and wants.

Speak from the perspective of your existing and prospective customers. Help employees bridge the gap between being productive and serving customers or clients.

Engage all employees in learning about and hearing from customers or clients. Bring employees into customer or client meetings and share messages and your customers' priorities.

Share sales targets and progress toward those targets with all employees. Speak of sales as if the company's future depends on it. It does.

Connect employee compensation with sales through profit sharing or bonuses based on new customers acquired and new businesses closed.

Essentially, it would help if you viewed yourself as the champion for your customers or clients. See your primary objective as helping all employees, most of whom have never been exposed to sales or the customer, and recognize the importance of serving and supporting your customers and how they play a role in such.

EMBRACE YOUR CHAMPIONS (THEY ARE THE KEY TO YOUR SUCCESS)

Champions will emerge as you share this message and help employees make these connections. These employees outside sales grasp your messages, embrace their impact on existing and new customers, and help spread your message. Engage these people on an individual level and solicit their support. Equip them with more information, knowledge, and direct exposure to your customers or clients, which will further solidify their newly adopted views and perspectives. It doesn't matter their department or how long they've been with the company. These early adopters are vital to helping you expand your message and influence more of your employees who will likely remain on the fence about this new "direction" or "priority" you share.

If you aren't an executive in a company and have picked up this book for ideas on multiplying your sales numbers, the same rules apply. You see, being a leader has nothing to do with your title, and you can take the same steps described above, regardless of your level of authority. In this instance, however, your greatest challenge will be to influence senior executives to understand the importance of your mission. Over time, as you engage others and demonstrate a sales-centric culture's positive influence on sales results, you'll gain their support and buy-in. You might even land yourself a promotion!

Before we go any further, you'd be right if you think that influencing a sales culture is a lot of work. However, you should realize that hundreds of companies have adopted a sales culture without any influence from the sales department. These organizations have recognized that sales are a company's lifeblood, and in turn, everyone who directly and indirectly influences the customer should realize the importance of and be skilled at supporting continued sales efforts.

Here are a few companies you may encounter whose focus is on a sales-centric culture. Sometimes, these companies need to have salespeople in a traditional sales role, whereas in other cases, salespeople handle the more significant (often commercial) transactions.

Carvana – an online used car retailer that provides an exceptional experience for their buyers without a direct sales team.

Atlassian – a custom software developer once suggested they had acquired 100,000 customers without a sales team.

Wells Fargo – a well-known US bank that has moved away from aggressive sales targets to improve its culture (and their sales haven't declined as a result).

Ritz Carlton – a hotel chain providing a luxurious experience for all its customers by empowering frontline employees to address any concerns their customers bring forward.

Although these companies are all very different, they have one thing in common. They rely on something other than their sales team to make all their sales; instead, they build a culture that enables additional selling opportunities. The sales multiplier framework is at work!

If you are up for the challenging work of building your sales-centric culture, then the only thing that will keep you focused on your mission is results, most notably the volume and frequency upon which new sales are generated. With this in mind, let's talk about how to compel employees outside of the sales department to recognize sales as the only measure that should matter.

As mentioned previously, influencing your organization's culture is no small feat. It's akin to turning a ship, meaning it can take a lot of effort and a very long time to begin to see that you are heading in the right direction. Nonetheless, every ship can be turned, and every culture can be influenced to recognize the value of sales.

First, it's essential to recognize that our goal isn't to get everyone to sell; instead, we are attempting to gain their support in identifying new opportunities to sell. This is an important distinction.

In a recent Global State of Sales Report, LinkedIn found that 88% of B2B buyers buy from those they perceive to be Trusted Advisors.[2] Unfortunately, however, when it came to assessing the "trustworthiness" of salespeople, the same study found that only 32% of those same buyers felt that salespeople were trustworthy.

The study's findings about "trust" shed light on an essential and often overlooked point. Salespeople are placed in building trust with our customers or clients. Still, the departments outside sales with which our customers or clients interact can determine how effective initial trust-building can be. In other words, you are only one poorly written response email to a customer or possibly one missed phone call from a client during their time of need away from disintegrating the trust that was so delicately built.

Many years ago, I developed my *Trusted Advisor Training Program*, where I work with teams across organizations that aren't directly involved in sales, helping them recognize and adopt new methods of interacting with customers or clients and influencing sales. In the program, we delve into the influence employees can have in re-selling customers and supporting upsells, cross-sells, and referrals. The program is a powerful way to shift the perspectives of those employees outside of sales in how their role influences the customer and, ultimately, the company's long-term success.

As an example, I recently worked with a Managed Service Provider (MSP) to help their technicians whose focus is to quickly resolve tickets issued by clients who require technical support. One of the objectives was to help the techs recognize the value of making recommendations on improvements in their client's IT networks and then share those same recommendations with the Business Development department. The methods we introduced were designed to ensure the MSP's clients were much more receptive to their "recommendations" and eager to speak with business development about how they can make the recommended changes. It created an entirely different dynamic for both the client and business development, all because clients believed that the technicians supporting them were their "Trusted advisors."

I've also worked with Customer Service, Production, and Operations teams across various sectors, including Industrial, Transportation,

Mining, Insurance, Technologies, Manufacturing, Construction, Banking, and Automotive.

You don't need my help to introduce or run such a program to achieve the same intent in your company. Identify all the different ways each department interacts with your customers or clients today and the influence those interactions can (and do) have on your customers' desire to stay, buy, and refer. Then, introduce improved methods and behaviors for those interactions, clearly defining the benefits engaging in these new methods or behaviors would have for each department (and everyone within the department).

In using this method to influence your company's culture, you seek to achieve a common realization among those participating that every interaction and conversation they have with customers or clients represents an opportunity to influence the future of that relationship. By being recognized as a trusted advisor, employees can positively impact their customer or client experience and open new opportunities to serve and support those customers.

The second point to mention here is that you will only reach some of your employees. There are too many people who don't work in sales or have never worked in sales and who (often as a result) do not want to be involved in sales. Wasting time attempting to influence everyone, particularly those without interest in sales, will be exhausting and defeating. Instead, focus your attention on those who recognize and adopt new behaviors. Place your energy and time into furthering their adoption of the latest Sales Multiplier methods we've discussed and share their success broadly. If you apply the Pareto Principle, likely 20% of the people you share these new methods with will likely quickly adopt and use them, whereas 80% won't be responsive. Keep in mind that just because it will seem like most people aren't responding to your new ideas or methods, the reality is that 60% of that 80% are sitting on the fence, waiting to see what will happen before they decide. So, if you share the wins and successes of those who adopt early (the initial 20%), then you'll also indirectly sway those who are fence-sitters. This is called the 20/60/20 Rule, a standard view in Change Management. Figure 9.1 demonstrates how this works.

The third tip I'll share with you here is providing you with a starting point to launch your efforts to influence your culture. Over my years of working with companies to build a more sales-centric culture, I've learned that the size of the company matters. How you go about influencing

Employees' Interest in Supporting Sales		
	FULLY COMMITTED	20%
	FENCE-SITTERS	60%
	NOT INTERESTED	20%

FIGURE 9.1
80/20 – with 60% of the 80% being fence-sitters

departments to adopt your new sales multiplier strategies in a small company (i.e., less than 20 employees) is very different than in a large company (i.e., >200 employees). The steps below shares the starting point for four companies of various sizes, from minor to enterprise. You can use this as the starting point, presuming you can execute this as a leader or executive within the company. I'll share a slightly different starting point below if you are a salesperson with little to no authority.

STEPS TO INTRODUCE YOUR SALES-CENTRIC CULTURE

Small Business (2–20 employees):

1. Identify the contact points various employees have with customers or clients.
2. Introduce the Sales Multiplier Framework (share employee benefits).
3. Give examples of how various employee roles impact the framework.
4. Work with everyone to identify touchpoints and develop scripts.

Medium-sized Company (21–200 employees):

1. Identify the contact points various departments have with customers or clients.
2. Introduce the Sales Multiplier Framework (share benefits to the company).
3. Give examples of how various roles impact the framework.
4. Introduce a trial with a specific department.

Large-sized Company (201–500 employees):

1. Identify the department with the most interactions with customers or clients.
2. Introduce the Sales Multiplier Framework (share benefits to the company).
3. Give examples of how the department is involved with the framework.
4. Work toward a trial with an individual within the department.

Enterprise (>500 employees):

1. Identify a single group within a department that interacts frequently with customers or clients.
2. Introduce the Sales Multiplier Framework (share benefits to the company).
3. Give examples of how individuals within the group influence the framework.
4. Work toward a test, work with the group, and share results with other groups in the same department.

It's important to mention that every company is unique, so these represent starting points for your efforts, not the entire strategy. If you have other ideas, however, given your knowledge of your organization's existing culture, then test them out. Your goal, as mentioned, is to focus on influencing the 20% of people who are interested and excited by your Sales Multiplier Formula, sharing the benefits and opportunities it provides to both the company and them.

INFLUENCING A SALES-CENTRIC CULTURE (WHEN YOU HAVE NO AUTHORITY)

Since the word "culture" can seem daunting to some, let me give you some perspective. The goal of your efforts outlined in this chapter is to "enlist the support of others to participate in your Sales Multiplier Formula." It's simple enough, so don't think for a moment that shifting or influencing your culture is beyond your pay scale or out of reach, considering your level of authority.

Additionally, as mentioned above, you don't need to sway everyone's opinion, nor do you need everyone to buy into your mission. If you need more authority, the time, or the desire to develop your strategy to influence your culture to be more sales-focused, don't. Apply the steps outlined above as your starting point and focus your energy on the individuals you consistently interact with.

For example, if you work with Jennifer in Customer Service most often and Bob in Accounts Receivable, spend time sharing some simple scripts to use when speaking with your customers or clients. Please don't discuss the Sales Multiplier Formula entirely, and don't share your desire to have a more sales-centric culture. Ask for their assistance and share examples of what they could do or say to assist you.

When you have little to no authority or desire to influence the overall culture of your organization, apply the KISS method and focus on introducing tactical steps to those who interact with your customers. Some will support you, others will not; however, you'll still be further ahead than if you did nothing. Remember, action produces outcomes, and analysis produces information.

On the other hand, if you are attempting to engage a larger group and have some level of authority to influence the culture, then there are some common barriers you'll encounter and should be prepared for. Let's discuss what those barriers are and (most importantly) how to overcome them next.

BARRIERS TO INTRODUCING A SALES-CENTRIC CULTURE

The results are well worth the effort despite the challenges or barriers that building a more sales-centric culture may present. Even if you lack authority or influence over other departments, you alone can significantly influence your company's culture.

Outside of the pushback you will likely receive if you announce your desire for a more sales-centric culture, other less obvious barriers may arise. If you aren't prepared for them, those barriers can be like an iceberg to the Titanic, quickly sinking any hope of garnering support for your Sales Multiplier System.

Here are some common barriers you'll encounter, as well as steps you can take to overcome them and move forward with implementing your sales multiplier system.

Barrier #1: No authority to influence other departments based on your title or position

Solution: Focus on building one-to-one relationships and garnering the support of individuals within departments who indirectly or directly influence your customers. Build a small network of people who appreciate you and your perspective and who are willing to assist you in your mission.

Barrier #2: Leaders in your company who need to support a sales-centric culture

Solution:

1. Focus on leaders who recognize and support your vision of a sales-centric culture.
2. Engage them and their teams, providing them with the resources, scripts, and support discussed above.
3. Celebrate wins with these teams and view success as a team event (not the result of your singular efforts).

Barrier #3: A toxic culture uninfluenced by your views or perspectives

Solution: If the culture is genuinely toxic and you cannot influence it, then focus on what you can influence. Like barrier #1, build one-to-one relationships and make it easy for these individuals to assist you. Share scripts and other resources, and be incredibly thankful when your desired support is garnered. In a toxic culture, focus on what you can influence, not what you can't.

Barrier #4: Limited resources to support implementing your sales multiplier framework

Solution: Focus on what areas would create the most benefit for your customers or clients and focus your attention on implementing your framework. Set small goals and objectives and engage others from the perspective of making their jobs easier rather than adding more work to their already full plates.

Barrier #5: Limited capacity to influence other departments, as identified above

Solution: Like the solution for barrier #2, focus your attention and energy on the departments (and leaders within those departments) who support your desire to multiply sales and build a more robust sales culture. Speak in terms of steps and process changes rather than influencing culture.

Barrier #6: Inability to implement all aspects of your sales multiplier system

Solution: Although the sales multiplier system is precisely that, a system of steps and stages designed to work in unison and help you dramatically increase your sales, you can introduce some of the systems to experience the outcomes of more sales. So, if you find that Customer Service is supportive and willing to assist in introducing upsells and cross-sells to your customers but aren't able (or willing) to ask for referrals, then take what you can get. In other words, although the system I've shared with you is intended to be installed as a system, introduce what you can, as you can. Enlist the assistance of those who are willing to assist. You are much further ahead introducing some aspects of the framework than waiting to introduce the system.

Barrier #7: Your skills are holding you back from introducing the system

Solution: If you are unfamiliar with or need more skill to solicit upsells and cross-sells as part of your selling techniques, you'll likely be uncomfortable asking others to support your efforts. There is nothing to be embarrassed about. In my work with sales executives and teams over the last 15 years, soliciting upsells and cross-sells is a go-to strategy. Most sales professionals are happy to make the sale and never mind strategically positioning and recommending additional or complementary sales. I would recommend reading my book, *The Unstoppable Sales Machine*, and then, if necessary, investing in one of my programs to improve your selling skills. New skills breed new confidence and might be exactly what you need to introduce your sales multiplier system fully.

You may encounter other barriers; however, these are the most common. Make sure to continue visiting www.salesmultiplierbook.com for up-to-date resources that I will add to ensure you can get the most from your sales multiplier system.

Let's focus on designing a customized sales multiplier formula for you and your organization.

Sales Multiplier Mindset: Building a more sales-centric culture requires you shift the perspective of your employees to that of being a trusted advisor to your customers or clients.

NOTES

1 https://www.linkedin.com/business/sales/blog/b2b-sales/these-7-stats-shed-light-on-the-future-of-sales

2 Author's Note: If you do believe you need additional support, visit www.shawncasemore.com for more information on our training and programs to multiply your sales and shift toward a trusted advisor approach to selling.

10

Foundation: Design Your Sales Multiplier Formula

In the world of Formula 1 racing, the launch off the starting line is often the determining factor as to whether you'll win the race or not. Even if you've qualified first and start in the pole position, if the drivers in second, third, or even fifth have a better launch than you, there's a good chance you won't maintain your first-place position.

In this chapter, I will share the steps to launch your sales multiplier formula. Like Formula 1 racing, your ability to launch your formula successfully can be the sole determinant of whether you win the race to multiplying your sales or get beaten by your competitors. In other words, if you get your launch right, you'll win; however, mess it up, and the chances of your multiplying your sales to the extent possible quickly fade.

SET YOUR GPS: ASSESS YOUR POSITIONING AND OFFERS

When I was younger, traveling to a new city, state, or country required that time first be spent reading a map. It took time to identify the highways, towns, streets, and turns in the order you should take them to ensure you reached your desired destination. It was common to find cars parked along the side of the road or at rest stops, with the driver awkwardly holding a large paper map up in front of their face, attempting to determine where they were in their journey and what turns to take next. Global positioning system (GPS) has changed all of this, and now, of course, you can

DOI: 10.4324/9781003463962-13

view where you are relative to your destination at any time and with little to no effort.

Before you plan and take the steps necessary to launch your sales multiplier formula, you'll need to set your GPS. Your ability to multiply your sales will depend on where you are currently. For example, multiplying your sales will be if you launch a new product and sell it in a mature market, which will require a different plan than selling your product in a relatively new market with little to no competition.

Your GPS then (which, for our purposes, we'll refer to as your *Global Position in Sales*) is represented by your position in your market, considering your current products or services. It identifies where you are relative to your competition and, in turn, informs how you can set your product or service, your company, and yourself apart from those competitors. Think of this exercise as capturing a moment in time during which you identify where you are in the market and what you need to do to reach your desired destination of multiplying your sales.

To set your Global Position in Sales:

1. Take a piece of paper and draw three vertical lines on the page, from top to bottom.
2. On the far left, write down your existing products or services you sell regularly.
3. In addition, list anything that you offer your customers or clients today as part of the benefit of buying from you.

Here are some examples to consider:

Financial Investment Firm Offer Examples:

Specific investment products
Your methods to manage those investments
Access to real-time information for clients
Software that enables better investment decisions

Commercial Real Estate Offer Examples:

Unique or exclusive properties
Access to information about long-term property valuation
Partnerships with contractors or lawyers
Network of contractors with special rates for skills

CNC Machining Company Offer Examples:

Unique CNC methods or equipment
Quality assurance standards or certifications
Rapid turnaround or delivery of customer orders
Equipment or employee capabilities

You get the idea. Your goal in listing your products or services should extend beyond the product or service itself and include all the ways in which you typically compare (or your customers or clients compare you) against your competitors.

Next, write the following words along the top of each of the three remaining columns: *Common Place, Competitive Advantage, Distinctive.* Figure 10.1 identifies what this chart looks like once complete.

For a printable chart to use and complete this exercise, visit www. salesmultiplierbook.com

Next, list your competitors and their products or services. The goal here is to identify the products or services you regularly encounter while attempting to sell. With this list complete, return to your GPS document and reflect upon your products or services compared to what your

COMPETITIVE ASSESSMENT		
Common Place	Competitive Advantage	Distinctive
Product/Service #1		
Product/Service #2		
Product/Service #3		
Product/Service #4		
Product/Service #5		
Product/Service #6		

FIGURE 10.1
Three columns with labels as above

competition offers. Note how your product or service ranks against the competition in the appropriate column. To determine this, use the following as your definitions:

Common Place – most of your competition sells your product or service.
Competitive Advantage – your product or service is something few competitors offer.
Distinctive – your product or service is something no one else sells or offers.

Your goal with this exercise is to assess your position relative to your competition. Be honest with yourself here. If what you offer is commonplace and something offered by all or most of your competitors, then identify it as such on your GPS document. This will inform the steps we'll take to develop and build your sales multiplier framework.

With this complete, let's move to the next critical step by assessing the strengths and opportunities in your existing sales processes, methods, and approaches.

YOUR FORENSIC SALES AUDIT

> You've got to know where you've been and what you've done to recognize what you should do next.
>
> Shawn Casemore

In the earlier chapters, you've completed assessments for several parts of your market, existing sales processes, and competition. This is designed to help you set a baseline upon which we will improve by introducing your sales multiplier formula. How can you take these various assessments and bits of information you've collected and organize them in a way that is useful and can help you successfully introduce and launch your SMF? That's where your forensic sales audit comes into play!

We recently built a fence around our yard, partially for privacy and to ensure our dog Charlie remains in our yard. We completed a survey of our property before we dug the first fence post hole. We hired a local survey company that sent out two people with what appeared to be a large telescope sitting atop a stand. One of the individuals looked through the telescope while the other carried a large stick and measuring tape. They moved around our property, setting small flags on the lawn to mark our property line. Once the survey was completed, they submitted it to our local municipal office, which approved it and issued us a building certificate to construct the fence.

Attempting to build our fence without a survey would have been problematic where we live. Local municipalities are known to monitor construction, issue fines, and even demand construction be halted until proper surveys are completed. Although some residents find this unreasonable for something as simple as a fence or shed, a survey is the only way to ensure that whatever you construct doesn't infringe on surrounding property.

When building the fence, the questions of where to place the first fence post and how to lay the fence became our next challenge. For example, should our contractor build from our house toward the property line or from a corner toward the home? Which side should he complete first, or does it matter? Fortunately, our contractor was able to identify where to place the first fence post. The stages in which he'd build the fence on account of using the survey, which showed the grading of the property, identified easements and other obstacles to consider in construction, all to build the fence quickly, with the strength and structure that would ensure it lasts.

You aren't likely building a fence around your company, and a survey isn't likely to help. Still, we are going to conduct something similar that will inform you of the steps you'll take to launch your Sales Multiplier Formula in the most effective way possible. The assessment we'll complete is designed to uncover the effectiveness of your existing sales processes, methods, and technology, identifying both gaps and opportunities. What will also become evident is what is working well in generating additional sales for you today. Following its completion, you'll be able to pinpoint precisely where you should begin when you launch your Sales Multiplier Formula.

When I complete this for clients, I refer to it as my Forensic Sales Audit, which is an intensive deep dive into your current state of sales. You can also complete this audit on your own. Table 10.1 sets out the areas to audit, the ideal state of each focus area, the desired results, and the steps and

TABLE 10.1

Shawn's Forensic Sales Audit Overview

Audit Focus Area	Overview	Desired Results	Recommendations
Lead Generation	Speed, Quality, Consistency, and Readiness of leads generated by sales.	Are high-quality leads developed consistently that align with ideal customer persona?	Improvements required to improve speed, quality, and consistency of leads generated.
Sales Process	Application and performance of individual sales process steps.	Does the sales process support rapid conversion and closure of new leads generated?	Improvements to the sales process steps efficiency and/or effectiveness.
Opportunity Development	Speed and quality of opportunities developed across the entire sales team.	What is the quality of opportunities that are developed? How consistently are opportunities developed?	Improvements to the steps to develop and nurture new sales opportunities.
Lead Conversion	Speed at which new leads are converted to high margin sales.	How quickly are new leads and opportunities converted to sale?	Improvements to how leads are converted to increase speed and reduce lost opportunities.
Close Success Rate	Overall success rate for closing new sales, and quality of the sales closed.	How quickly are we closing deals, and how closely do those deals align with our ideal customer persona and margins?	Improve the quality and margin of deals closed.
Sales Team Performance	Effectiveness of the sales team both individually and collectively as it pertains to generating new business.	How well does everyone on the sales team perform? How well does the group collaborate to generate sales?	Improvements to skills and communications for individuals and the team to increase sales.
Sales Strategy	Quality and applicability of the sales strategy in achieving desired sales targets.	Does a current sales strategy exist? How well does it inform the goals and directions of the sales team?	Design, re-develop, or re-align the sales strategy to ensure it informs the key targets and activities of the sales team.
Sales Metrics	Leading and lagging measures for individuals and the sales team that inform performance.	Is there both leading and lagging performance measures? Are measures shared, understood, and applied to consistently improve performance?	Develop or re-set sales key performance indicators to ensure sales performance is monitored appropriately, and information attained is acted upon.

recommendations to address any gaps between where you are today and where you should be.

Although thorough, an audit of this magnitude is critical to ensuring a strong sales strategy, system, processes, and support for your sales multiplier formula. Gaps or issues in any of the above areas are most likely to lead to an inability to multiply your sales, for example:

Without a method for generating high-quality leads, you won't have the volume of sales opportunities to capitalize on your sales multiplier formula fully.

An insufficient or ineffective sales process may result in introducing your sales multiplier formula at inopportune times, resulting in a reduction rather than an increase in selling opportunities.

Low conversion rates of new sales mean that your conversion of upsells, cross-sells, and the obtaining of referrals will be less than ideal.

A low close ratio suggests gaps in your sales teams' closing methods and skills, and as a result introducing your sales multiplier formula might further reduce the size, frequency, and value of sales opportunities closed.

If your sales team is underperforming or lacks the skills and ability to achieve your sales targets, the chances of them successfully introducing your sales multiplier formula are low at best.

A lack of a sales strategy means a lack of direction for your sales team, and as a result, there will be little clarity on when and how to introduce your sales multiplier formula best to support your sales objectives.

If you don't have sufficient sales metrics in place, there will be no way to know the impact of your sales multiplier formula. Hence, the chances of your gaining benefits from its introduction are slim.

If you'd like to explore auditing and improving the performance of your existing sales methods and processes more deeply, read my book *The Unstoppable Sales Machine*. It provides a framework and tools for selling in the new economy.

For a printable version of the Forensic Sales Audit, visit www.sales multiplierbook.com.

INTRODUCE A MACHINE FOR UNSTOPPABLE SALES™

In the event your sales processes are not as strong as they could be, it may make sense for you to make improvements here, to ensure you are fully capitalizing on your sales multiplier formula. Your starting point in this case, considering the work you've done to assess your offers, and to uncover the strengths and vulnerabilities of your sales processes and systems, is to introduce a sales machine of sorts, or what I like to refer to as an Unstoppable Sales™ Machine.

Before we dive into this, consider a recent study conducted by Marketo[1], which found that the top communication channels through which today's B2B buyers engage with a brand or company are:

1. Visiting their website
2. Email
3. Online communities
4. Chat
5. Social media
6. Mobile Device/Apps
7. Podcasts/Webinars
8. Blogs
9. Video

What's most important from this research is not how today's buyers prefer to engage but what's driving this behavior change. These can be summarized into three key behavior drivers: the continued expansion of technology and our acceptance of it, events such as the pandemic of 2020 that influenced buying behavior, and, of course, the demographic of today's buyers.

Despite these shifts toward more digital interactions, relationships still matter. What's changed is how buyers prefer to engage to build relationships. The adage, "people only buy from those they know, like, and trust," remains, so whether you are selling face-to-face, virtually, or via the telephone, the goal is to use the communication channels that help build trust and attract a steady flow of new and ideal prospects to us.

In my book *The Unstoppable Sales Machine*, I explain exactly how to build and introduce a process that achieves this purpose and becomes self-sustaining, like a machine of sorts. There are seven components you need to create to build your very own unstoppable sales^{SM} machine, as described below.

THE SEVEN COMPONENTS OF YOUR UNSTOPPABLE SALES^{SM} MACHINE

Component #1: Magnetic Attraction

Most businesses' greatest failure is the failure to have proven methods in place that attract new buyers on a continuum. Instead, there seem to be three different positions sales leaders take, namely:

1. The attraction of new buyers is the sole responsibility of marketing.
2. Prospecting activities by the sales team are sufficient to attract new buyers.
3. New buyers will naturally emerge as awareness of a company's brand grows.

These views are necessarily wrong, but individually, more is needed to attract the constant flow of new buyers your business needs to grow. Every new customer has a life cycle through which they move. This life cycle will differ depending on what you're selling, but the main message is that a new customer will only last for a while. Therefore, we need to find methods that continuously attract new buyers for the following reasons:

- A steady flow of new leads that keep our opportunity pipe full.
- Creates opportunities to sell to new buyers, allowing us to shed those customers who no longer fit our ideal buyer profile.
- Ability to scale up sales when we want or need to.
- We have increased our ability to control pricing and profit margins.
- Ensures our sales team (and supporting departments) remain on their toes and eager for new opportunities.
- Provides us with better stability and control over future sales and customers.

This is the first component of your machine because without a system in place to attract new ideal buyers continuously, there is no machine.

Component #2: Pattern Interrupt

If I were to yell "Fire!" I'd only have your complete attention for a matter of seconds. Plenty of articles have been written to dispute the slow decline of our attention span and ability to focus. If you want to test this theory, how many pages of this book have you read (or listened to) before you glanced at your phone or responded to a text or email?

Considering our ability to focus is diminishing, your ability to capture and retain a buyer's attention long enough to share the value your product or service can provide them is also diminishing. When was the last time you had the opportunity to have the undivided attention of your buyer for more than 60 minutes?

For this reason, once you have garnered your buyer's attention, the second component of your machine is to provide them with something that interrupts their expectations and engages them.

To attract a buyer's attention is one thing, but to keep it requires an interruption that snaps them out of their routines and garners their attention and interest. In this section of the book, we'll look at numerous successful pattern interrupt strategies to deploy to get just enough of your buyer's time to ensure they are clear on the value your product or service can offer them.

Component #3: Real-time Responsiveness

When was the last time you attempted to reach a company with a question and successfully connected with someone (who knew what they were talking about)? If you reach out via an online chat, the first message you'll likely receive is *"no one is available right now."* If you attempt to call a customer service or sales number, you will likely be directed to a voicemail system that tells you to be patient because *"call volumes are higher than normal."*

Let's take a quick look at an example.

I recently contacted a few dealers in my local area to inquire about a new vehicle. My wife and I had narrowed it down to three different models, so I contacted three different dealers (directly to someone in sales) to inquire about a trade-in value and inventory availability.

> Dealer #1: The salesperson responded several days later, requesting that I bring the car to their dealership so their sales manager could "Take a look."

Dealer #2: The salesperson responded two days later, apologizing for their late response, and asking some further questions, which it took another two days for them to reply to once shared.

Dealer #3: The salesperson responded within an hour and then moved to text messaging, where she provided a trade value (dependent on a review of the car), several vehicle options, and different payment terms and options. All this was completed over a two-day span.

Who do you think we purchased a vehicle from? The salesperson at dealer #3 was the most responsive. Where all else is the same, responding first to an inquiry can be the difference between making the sale and not.

We've already discussed how today's buyers give sales so little of their time; the last thing you want to do is miss them when they are ready to engage. For this reason, the third component in your Unstoppable Sales Machine is enabling a Real-Time Response, or RTR for short. Think of this as your secret weapon to dominate your competition. Wherever your potential buyer is, you want to be there and are ready to respond.

Component #4: Lead with Value

When you consider how much time today's buyers spend researching solutions *before* engaging with sales, the obvious question becomes how to engage with them when doing their research.

The answer is by providing VALUE.

According to the Merriam-Webster dictionary, value is "a relevant, worth, utility or importance." With this in mind, a buyer's values can differ depending on where they are in their buyer's journey. For this reason, we must look at the value of each of the five stages along their journey to define what we might offer to gain attention, interest, and engagement.

Our Unstoppable Sales™ Machine aims to provide value for your buyer at each level of this pyramid based on their needs and expectations. The more value you can provide, the faster you'll engage your buyers and move them toward the close.

If you doubt that value can significantly impact a buyer or be a differentiator in your market, think again.

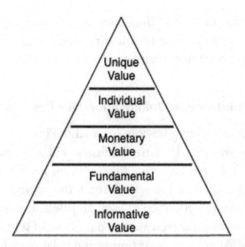

FIGURE 10.2
The Five Levels of Buyer Value

How can Starbucks, for example, offer a cup of coffee at a price that is at least double or triple that of its closest competitors? By providing value to its buyers.

More specifically, the value that Starbucks offers over its competitors include:

- The unique experience they provide.
- The atmosphere they offer.
- Their product has a wide variety of options that allow their buyers to customize.
- Their unique branding (to this day, I can't figure out why a "tall americano" is small?).
- Unique benefits of being a Starbucks customer (i.e., Starbucks rewards).

You might look at this list and say, "Okay, Shawn, but some of these features are the same as Starbucks competitors offer." Yes, but value is something you stack, and the more you can add that is helpful, relevant, and useful to your buyer, the better chance you'll have to stand out. So, although Starbucks's rewards might be "competitive value," the atmosphere they offer is "unique" in their market.

We'll discuss this further in the following chapters, but for now, know that your ability to build your machine relies on your ability to uncover and present what your buyers value most.

Component #5: Introduce Qualification Hurdles

I was never great at running track in high school but did okay at the hurdles. The reason was that I wasn't the fastest kid at school, but to compete (and win!) at the Hurdles, you didn't want or need to be the quickest. Instead, winning at the Hurdles was all about timing and balance. Picking the right speed ensured you cleared each Hurdle and positioned yourself during the landing to get a pre-calculated number of steps before the next Hurdle. Those who could get their timing and balance right were the most likely to make it to the end in record time and without knocking a hurdle over.

Like the Hurdles, the priority when developing new sales opportunities is not how quickly you can connect with buyers to generate new leads but the quality of the leads you generate.

Your success depends on five factors:

1. Understanding precisely who your ideal buyer is.
2. Your ability to find and connect with these ideal buyers.
3. How well you engage the buyer when you do connect.
4. The degree to which the buyer finds value in the connection.
5. Where the buyer is in their journey when you connect.

For this reason, spending equal time on every inquiry or lead that comes your way is ludicrous. Instead, we must be hyper-focused on spending time with our ideal buyers.

To do so, we need to introduce what I refer to as Qualification Hurdles. Each buyer must pass through these stages in the buying process to reach the next level. With hurdles in place, you can allocate your most important resource (your time) to the customers who stand out and match your ideal buyer criteria.

We'll discuss the specifics of each Hurdle in the coming chapters, but for now, Figure 10.3 represents an overview of the Qualification Hurdle process we'll be introducing.[2]

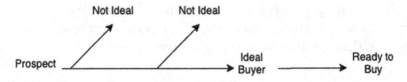

FIGURE 10.3
Buyer Qualification Hurdles

Component #6: Evangelistic Customers

Aside from referrals, your existing customers are your shortest and easiest route to generating new sales. Unfortunately, too many companies ignore their current customers, dismissing them as a source of new business aside from the odd referral.

That's the wrong mindset.

Instead of thinking, "I already have their business," you should think, "How can I get more business from my current clients or customers?" Here are a few examples of how you can capture more business from your current clients or customers:

Ten Ways to Gain More Business from Existing Clients or Customers:

1. Obtain written recommendations.
2. Provide video testimonials.
3. Obtain case studies that you can share with new buyers.
4. Provide introductions to their trade associations.
5. Introduce you to their peer networks or professional groups.
6. Help you find opportunities to speak at relevant conferences or events.
7. Share their favorable experiences with your company across their social networks.
8. Collaborate with you on a presentation or article.
9. Send your marketing materials to their network.
10. I recommend that you join professional networks to gain access to more buyers.

In addition to these opportunities, your buyers' needs evolve and change daily. Combining this with your company's ever-expanding services and capabilities creates new opportunities to work together!

When creating Unstoppable Sales, you must consistently connect with, educate, and add value to your existing client or customer base. It is one of the critical mechanisms by which you'll generate new sales.

Component #7: Customer Allure

The last component in your Unstoppable Sales[SM] Machine is Customer Allure. Many companies attempt to start their journey here, hiring a marketing firm to find them new buyers when it's the last thing they should do.

To this point, we've defined who the ideal buyer is that your sales team should be pursuing, methods to interrupt and garner their attention, what they might value from interacting with us, and how we might offer that value. We've also put in place methods to ensure we invest our time only with those buyers who match our ideal buyer profile.

After all, you don't want to attract just any client but rather more of your ideal clients.

As a result, you will create customer allure once you have the rest of your machine up and running.

The components of Customer Allure include the following:

1. Clarify our ideal buyer's needs and wants.
2. A method to continuously provide value.
3. Qualification Hurdles launched.
4. Successful Sales Funnel in action.
5. Automation to support scaling.
6. Marketing Resource Construction.

With the rest of your machine fully operational and underway, you are in the best possible position to introduce Customer Allure and capitalize on any investment of time or money you make in marketing.

With the steps above forming the foundation of your sales process, when you add on the sales multiplier formula and engage other employees in your mission to multiply your sales, it's easy to see just how weak your sales strategy, processes, and methods are today.

Aside from having an effective sales process, it would help if you also built a strong sales team to execute the process. After all, they are on the front lines of everything we've discussed and will be the champions to help you launch your sales multiplier formula.

To strengthen your sales team to higher levels of performance, you'll need to provide them with the right skills, knowledge, and expertise to set you apart from your competition. As you might imagine, there is a formula for doing so ... and I wrote a book about this too!

BUILD A SALES TEAM THAT IS UNSTOPPABLE

Reading, studying, and researching are all critical in becoming high-performing sales professionals, but ultimately, we learn by doing.

If you are a sales leader, building an Unstoppable Sales Team that supports and embraces your Sales Multiplier Formula requires you to create a sales culture that embraces learning by testing and trying new skills, techniques, and strategies. Our studies have shown that most sales professionals follow their organization's sales process almost to a tee for fear of being reprimanded or frowned upon if they don't produce the desired sales results. Although having a sales process and practices makes sense, it creates several challenges:

1. It doesn't allow employees to be creative (i.e., exploration of new methods and techniques given someone's strengths).
2. Employees can't practice individuality (i.e., adjustments to methods to better align with individual behavioral preferences).
3. It reinforces conformity, which will, over the long term, further stifle creativity and the desire to adjust methods based on changes in buyer behaviors and expectations.

In other words, sales professionals need freedom to apply sales processes. Although following proven practices to sell makes sense, this needs to account for each salesperson's individuality.

As you might imagine, environments that emulate the "do it our way or hit the highway" approach in how they expect their sales team to operate are neither motivating enough to keep strong sales performers nor enticing enough to attract new talent.

So, the keys to forming a foundation for your unstoppable sales team are as follows:

1. Create an environment where your sales team feels comfortable and confident sharing new strategies and ideas.
2. Provide your team with the opportunity to test and trial new methods without fear, reprimand, or embarrassment.
3. Ensure the team openly shares their successes or lessons learned with other team members.
4. New steps or lessons learned are incorporated into existing practices or processes to ensure the sales team consistently uses them.

My Sales Team Performance Framework depicted in Figure 10.4 shows how the Learn by Doing practice should be incorporated to build your Unstoppable Sales Team.

Creating an environment such as this motivates the sales team. They have processes that, if followed, have historically led to solid sales results, but they can also test and trial new theories, first discussing them with their team for input and feedback.

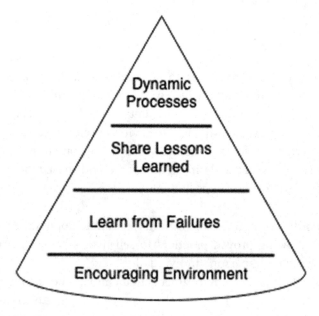

FIGURE 10.4
The Sales Team Performance Framework

The indirect result is consistently improving sales results for the entire team and an encouraging environment where employees believe their ideas are essential and have a platform to share them.

With an effective sales process in place and a team structured and ready to sell successfully, let's focus on the initial steps you'll need to take to launch your sales multiplier formula.

Sales Multiplier Mindset: The sales multiplier formula is not a sales process, but rather a series of strategies, steps, and tactics you can add onto your existing sales process. When matched with a process like the Unstoppable Sales™ Machine, your sales will be literally unstoppable.

NOTES

1 https://www.marketingcharts.com/customer-centric/customer-engagement-79971
2 Author's Note: Stage six in The Unstoppable Sales™ Machine introduces Rocket Fuel Referrals, which we discussed in an earlier chapter as a component of your Sales Multiplier Formula. If you apply the steps and methods discussed earlier, you can skip this step and move to developing Evangelistic Customers.

11

Testing: Implement Your New Sales Multiplier Formula

Some of you, eager to jump right into multiplying your sales, have likely skipped this chapter. If this sounds like you, then I've got some great news! In this chapter, we'll dive right into implementation.

Before we dive in, however, heed the following warning. Launching your sales multiplier formula (SMF) without doing the prep work laid out in the previous chapters (i.e., gaining other team members' support in identifying opportunities, developing scripts for those team members to use, designing the steps to ensure your SMF works as you intend) will result in lackluster results. If you have already been attempting to close upsells or cross-sells and haven't been seeing the results you expect, it's likely the lack of preparatory work laid out in earlier chapters is the reason. If referrals have been something you've been pursuing with little success, it's likely because you need to follow the steps I laid out in the earlier chapters. So, fair warning: do the prep work, or you won't like to experience the results you expect.

INTRODUCE YOUR SALES MULTIPLIER FORMULA

Hopefully, by now, you've noticed that the SMF isn't a sales process like the one I describe in my book *The Unstoppable Sales Machine*. Rather, it's a method that you can add to your existing sales process. Consider it like adding a turbocharger to your already high-performance engine. It will help you further multiply your sales.

The objective is to take your existing sales process, assuming it is somewhat effective in generating new sales, and then add the SMF. If you do so, then you'll multiply your sales.

DOI: 10.4324/9781003463962-14

Designing your new formula requires you to follow and apply ten steps, which I've laid out below. Think of this as your roadmap to transitioning from how you sell today to incorporating the various stages and steps to multiply your sales that we've discussed to date. The steps are demonstrated in Figure 11.1 and further explained below.

SHAWN'S TEN STEPS TO INTRODUCE YOUR SALES MULTIPLIER FORMULA

1. Map out the steps in your existing sales process (i.e., initial meeting, presentation, discovery dialogue, proposal shared).
2. Identify the upsell and cross-sell options you intend to share with customers or clients. (These can be existing or new, or a combination of both. If they are new, ensure you've validated their worth and value with existing clients or customers.)
3. Identify the different roles (and individuals) within your company who directly and indirectly interact with your customers (i.e., customer service, engineering, operations).
4. Using your existing sales process steps identified, determine at what points the various upsell and cross-sell options could be presented. Next to each of these, identify who might first mention them by department.
5. Design scripts for use by departments outside of sales to assist them with mentioning or introducing your upsell and cross-sell options.
6. Meet with each department to share the sales process and identify where the upsell and cross-sell options come into play. Introduce these scripts for that department you identified in step #3 above and request their support in introducing these options at the appropriate time (based on their interactions with your customer or client).
7. Map out your customer or client journey (i.e., what they experience as steps and interactions with your company).
8. Identify the points at which a referral would be mentioned or requested and the appropriate language during these interactions. Break these down as follows:
   a. Pre-sale: seeding initial conversations with the future request for a referral if your customer or client is satisfied.

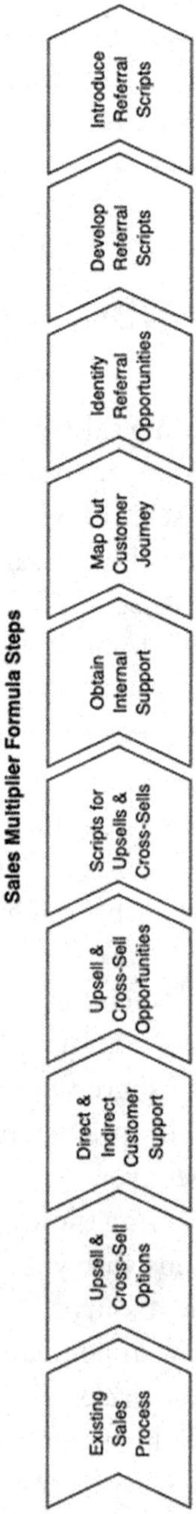

Sales Multiplier Formula Steps

| Existing Sales Process | Upsell & Cross-Sell Options | Direct & Indirect Customer Support | Upsell & Cross-Sell Opportunities | Scripts for Upsells & Cross-Sells | Obtain Internal Support | Map Out Customer Journey | Identify Referral Opportunities | Develop Referral Scripts | Introduce Referral Scripts |

FIGURE 11.1

Design your Sales Multiplier Formula

b. At sale: mention the value of a referral and the options for sharing it at the time of the sale.
c. Post-sale: Request the referral at various intervals after the sale.
d. Lost customer: requesting a referral as part of your "staying in touch" strategy with past clients.

9. Identify the different departments that interact with your customers or clients at these stages and develop scripts for them to use as part of their interactions.

10. Introduce the different stages of referral requests and scripts to each department identified in step #9 above, soliciting their buy-in and support in supporting your referral requests.

These steps should be straightforward, as they are intended to be. Whether you lead the company or the sales team or simply work in sales, identifying the what, how, and when to introduce your new upsells and cross-sells isn't all that challenging. Neither is developing your strategy for asking for referrals.

Beyond introducing these steps, the challenge will be in gaining the buy-in and support of the additional departments and people to support your sales multiplier framework. The main ingredient to gaining buy-in will be to create a compelling reason for the support of others. As mentioned, selling is often considered something only those in sales participate in. Aside from introducing the steps or stages, your job is to change or at least shift their perspective.

To assist you with developing compelling reasons to support your new sales multiplier framework, I've shared a list of example statements you can choose from (or modify) for various departments below. Feel free to apply these in your situation to assist in gaining the support of others.

COMPELLING REASONS FOR NON-SALES DEPARTMENTS TO SUPPORT YOUR SALES MULTIPLIER FORMULA

Compel Customer Service to Support Your SMF

You interact with our customers/clients more often than sales.
The relationships you build in supporting our customers/clients put you in the best position to make valuable upsell or cross-sell recommendations.

When you follow up with our customers/clients, just include this question (insert upsell, cross-sell, or referral request here).

Let's add a referral request to your email signature file, making it easy for customers/clients to make the introduction.

Compel Finance or Accounting to Support Your SMF

When you follow up with questions about billing, can you include this question (insert upsell, cross-sell, or referral request here)?

When you set up a new customer/client account, can you make this upsell or cross-sell suggestion?

If a customer or client is late on their payments after you assist them in finding a solution, can you make this referral request?

Compel Operations to Support Your SMF

When you speak to the client while setting up their account, mention when we'll be following up to request a referral.

If a client reaches out to resolve an issue, once the problem is solved, always ask about a referral using this script.

When creating the customer/client's profile, make any of these cross-sell or upsell recommendations based on what they've invested in.

Compel Production to Support Your SMF

When you call to arrange product shipment, use this script to ask about a referral.

When the customer visits our facility to audit the process, make sure you show them the upsell or cross-sell options.

If the customer calls to confirm the order details or quality, mention our desire for referrals from our best customers.

The key to overcoming resistance any departments outside of sales may have in supporting your new sales efforts is to make it easy for them to provide support. Although I've used some vague scripts here for demonstration purposes, they provide you with a starting point to do so. Identify those departments with whom you need support, then meet with them to discuss the support required. By using these scripts, you are answering the most common questions you'll encounter when trying to engage others to support your formula: "What should I say?" and "When should I say it?"

When you approach the support of others in this manner, you remove the "work" or effort to support your SMF (which also reduces complaints or excuses). Further, you eliminate any errors or missteps that might occur when you leave the presentation of upsells, cross-sells, and referral solicitation under the complete control of the other departments.

INTRODUCE FEEDBACK LOOPS TO GAUGE PROGRESS

When delivering one of my customized sales training programs, I solicit feedback at the end of each module and the program's end from both participants and the executives that bring me in. Having these "feedback checkpoints" ensures that I can consistently gain insights into improvements that will continue improving the training and the speed by which participants develop, for example, how effective a specific model was in explaining a process or method or if a role-play helped address weaknesses in a discovery dialogue or negotiation.

Feedback from your existing customers or clients, done at the right time and with the right questions, is critical to continuously improving your systems, methods, scripts, and processes. In this instance, they'll be vital in ensuring our SMF is practical and achieves the desired results.

By soliciting feedback and using the intelligence gained from it to make minor adjustments (where it makes sense to do so), you not only improve your sales methods but also create a level of stickiness with your customers, who appreciate your attempt to ensure their experience and results achieve their objectives.

As described below, there are three keys to soliciting feedback from your customers or clients to support your SMF.

Shawn's Keys for Effective Customer Feedback Loops

1. Be transparent about the feedback you need.

   The key to effectively soliciting feedback is to be transparent with customers about what feedback you seek and why it's important to both you (to improve their overall experience) and them (to improve the impact your company, its products, or services can have). For example, you might ask for their feedback on your presentation of an upsell or whether the request made for a referral was at the right time, making it easy for the customer to consider and support.

2. Choose the correct times to solicit feedback.

   In sales, there's an old saying that suggests "timing is everything." Soliciting feedback is no different. You would only ask for feedback on the effectiveness of a referral request after you ask for the referral, and you should wait to ask. The best approach would be to wait a week, follow up to see if your customer or client has identified a potential referral, and if they haven't, ask whether your approach to requesting a referral was the right time or if there might have been a better method to do so. Timing is everything.

3. Be specific in your request for feedback.

   If a new product, service, or step in your sales process doesn't land as it should, your existing customers, with whom you have already built trust and confidence, will tell you. To get the most from their feedback then, ask specific questions. For example, "Was my request for a referral good?" is not exact and is likely to lead to nothing substantive. More specificity in the ask would lead to a more beneficial outcome, for example: "I asked you for a referral, provided you a week to think about it, then followed up. Do you think I could have approached this differently, which would have made it easier for you to provide a referral?"

Examples of Critical Customer Feedback to Solicit

When it comes to ensuring the effectiveness of your SMF, every level can and should be tested with existing customers or clients before you launch fully. This feedback can provide valuable insights into improvements or changes in your methods, scripting, and processes; demonstrate whether your new methods for upselling and cross-selling are effective; and determine whether referrals are likely to be obtained.

Here are some examples of feedback you can and should obtain from your customers in support of launching and improving your SMF:

1. Do the upsells and cross-sells add value to your customer's investment? What value do they provide both quantitively and qualitatively?
2. Is your presentation and scripting effective? If not, what changes should be made?

3. Does the timing of the introduction make sense to your customer? Is there a better time to introduce cross-selling or upselling?
4. Does the person who may have introduced the concept of an upsell or cross-sell make sense to the customer? If not, who else would be best to make this introduction?
5. Does your method for soliciting referrals have sufficient influence to make your customer want to make an introduction or referral recommendation?

Gain customer feedback at every stage of your SMF. This will ensure that your introduction, methods, process, and scripting have the impact you expect and need to multiply your sales.

PHASING IN YOUR SALES MULTIPLIER FORMULA

To this point, I'm presuming you've completed your forensic sales audit as described above and introduced feedback checkpoints to obtain ideas, input, and improvements to ensure your products, services, approaches, methods, and processes of your SMF are all effective. So now what?

I realize that by this point, you're likely thinking that you'll be overwhelmed by information, so let me put you at ease by laying out the steps you'll take to phase in your SMF.

Sales Multiplier Formula Implementation Plan

Step 1: Complete Your Forensic Sales Audit
Begin by auditing your existing sales process, methods, and practices using the chart from earlier in this chapter. Once complete, review the results to identify opportunities for improvement. Prioritize these improvements based on their ability to assist you in improving upsell, cross-sell, and referral opportunities.

Step 2: Introduce Customer Feedback Loops (for ongoing intelligence and improvement)
Begin soliciting feedback from your existing (long-term) customers or clients by introducing customer feedback loops using the steps outlined above.

Step 3: Introduce or Improve Your Upsells

Whether you have existing upsells or not, the steps you'll follow here remain the same except for the first step.

1. Identify complimentary upsells for your existing customers or clients.
2. Review existing upsells and assess their value to the customer. What changes are necessary?
3. What measures should you take to assess uptake for upsells?
4. Who is best involved in the introduction of upsells? How will you introduce them?
5. What scripts can you provide to assist in their introduction or mention?
6. How can you pilot your new upsell process and scripts? For how long?
7. Once launched, how will you ensure those identified by other departments as interested in upsells are captured and transitioned to sales?
8. How frequently will you review upsells for interest, impact, and improvements?

Step 4: Introduce or Improve Your Cross-Sells

The steps to improve your cross-sells are virtually the same as the upsells listed above. Remember that if you have cross-sells already in place, then skip step #1 below:

1. Identify complimentary cross-sells for your existing customers or clients.
2. Review existing cross-sells and assess their value to the customer. What changes are necessary?
3. What measures should you take to assess uptake for cross-sells?
4. Who is best involved in the introduction of cross-sells? How will you introduce them?
5. What scripts can you provide to assist in their introduction or mention?
6. How can you pilot your new cross-sell process and scripts? For how long?
7. Once launched, how will you ensure those identified by other departments as interested in cross-sells are captured and transitioned to sales?
8. How frequently will you review upsells for interest, impact, and improvements?

Step 5: Introduce Your Referral System

Following the steps outlined in earlier chapters, the process for introducing your referral system is somewhat straightforward:

1. When should referrals be solicited from existing, past, and lost customers?
2. Who is in the best position to ask for or suggest referrals?
3. What scripts and steps are necessary to ensure the referral is requested?
4. How frequently will you review the referrals received to determine effectiveness?
5. What is your process for following up on referrals? How will you capture these?
6. What rewards will you give to those who provide a referral?
7. How often will you review your referral process and scripts to ensure effectiveness?

Step 6: Quarterly Review Process

The last step in implementing your SMF is to have a regular and repeating review process. Think of this like a sales meeting, with the sole intention of ensuring your upsells, cross-sells, and referral requests are effective and producing the additional sales you expect.

The agenda for your quarterly review process should consist of a review and discussion of each specific area, the results achieved, the obstacles or barriers encountered, and the further improvements expected to yield improved results. A sample agenda is listed below.

Sales Multiplier Formula Quarterly Meeting Agenda:

Review of new upsells and cross-sells made in the designated period.

Recognize those who have been involved (share best practices).

Discuss suggested changes or improvements in the upsell and cross-sell processes.

Discuss any changes to scripting, presentation, or involvement.

Set upsell and cross-sell targets for the coming month(s).

Review referrals received in the designated period.

Discuss any changes to method, scripting, presentation, or involvement.

Set referral targets for the coming months.

These are steps and methods to introduce and launch your SMF. If you'd like a more detailed guide, visit www.salesmultiplierbook.com.

SLOW THIS DOWN TO SPEED UP YOUR SALES

When I sold my first car in my early twenties, which was my first official job in sales (if you don't include my lawn care and snow removal business from my teen years), my excitement and eagerness to immediately make the next sale were almost unbearable. The experience of closing a sale today creates a similar, albeit less exciting, rush of adrenaline. My experience has told me that rushing toward the next sale can be a mistake. In other words, to be successful at selling anything, you'll need to walk before you run.

If there is something I've learned about sales as I've gained more experience (and aged), it's that thinking time between sales is as important as the sale itself. Running around closing deals is great, but stopping briefly to assess exactly what led to making the sale is critical to duplicate your success. Every sale you make will be different, with a different prospect, a different type of company, and different objections. Still, as you gain experience, you'll find fewer and fewer situations in which you'll need guidance on what to do.

You see, the goal in selling is to generate the greatest results (i.e., sales) with the least effort. When you do this, you limit the time from lead to sale and shorten your time to close. This is a critical measure for any salesperson or sales team, and it's a question to consistently consider, specifically, "How can we close the time to sale?"

Although most sales leaders, executives, and sales professionals recognize this, they need to realize that you need time to reflect on what's working and what's not to positively impact your time to sell.

Thinking time, or reflection time, whatever you prefer to call it, is the only means you must assess what's working and what's not. More importantly, this time allows you the opportunity to determine what changes, if any, are required to further your results.

There is a lot of work involved in putting together your sales multiplier system and rushing to the next sale or the next step will only allow you a little thinking time. Instead, start with one component, such as upsells, and fully introducing this component will enable you to assess how well it is working before you move to cross-sells. Suppose you approach the launch of your SMF differently. In that case, there is a risk you'll be faced with a burdensome series of process steps that need to achieve the immediate results you expect. Then you'll give up.

I'm sure you can see from what you've read to this point that the SMF will multiply your sales. It's as obvious as a peanut butter sandwich. However, the excitement around the opportunity can lead to a desire to overextend yourself and attempt to introduce multiple steps at once.

Instead, take a more systematic approach and purposefully inject some thinking time to fully assess what's working, what's not, and what needs to change. Here are some examples of where and how to introduce thinking time to fully evaluate your SMF efforts and results.

Now that we've discussed the importance of taking a systematic approach to introducing your SMF, let's talk about the future of sales and how your SMF will set up to win the race for new customers.

Sales Multiplier Mindset: After implementing the ten steps for your Sales Multiplier Formula, you will still need to engage others in support of your objectives for increased upsells, cross-sells, and referrals. Use the scripts provided to remove the "effort" for other departments from whom you need support.

12

Winning the Race for New Customers

When it comes to obtaining ongoing value from your sales multiplier formula over the long term, there are several factors we need to consider. First, what are the possible shifts in how buyers prefer to buy and interact with sales? How is technology influencing both buyers and sellers? How can you evolve your SMF if you want to continue increasing selling opportunities? In this chapter, we'll address all three of these points, and I'll share some final thoughts.

EVOLUTION OF TOMORROW'S CUSTOMER

A recent salesforce study suggested that 80% of customers now consider the company's experience as important as its products and services. This is not surprising when you consider that companies like Apple, Walmart, Amazon, and Starbucks are all known for being as obsessed with their customers' experience as they are with the quality of their products. The reason this statistic is important to embrace is simple. Well-thought-out upsells and cross-sells are a form of personalization.

When you follow the steps and methods laid out in this book, not only will you increase your Total Customer Sale Value (TCSV), but you will also increase the perception of personalization, which provides three significant benefits:

1. Increased Customer Retention: You'll keep customers for longer because they receive more value from your company and are more integrated and involved in additional sales.

DOI: 10.4324/9781003463962-15

2. Ease of Referrals: Your referral system will be more effortless to introduce and result in increased referrals because your customers will perceive the increased value they've attained from your company.
3. Increased Market Recognition: Your efforts will result in more customers sharing their positive experiences, which will increase word-of-mouth recognition and selling opportunities, all without spending on advertising.

I've used Apple products for years, mainly because of the ease of the overall experience. For example, when I purchased a new MacBook every few years, the product experience was like no other. When I receive the new MacBook, I open it up (it comes fully charged), set it near my existing MacBook, and then hit the power button. Once powered on, the first message on the screen will ask if I want to transfer all my information and profile from the existing MacBook (sitting nearby) to the new MacBook. After selecting "yes," the process is complete within a few minutes, and my new MacBook is ready to use.

Just visit apple.com and browse the menu, and you'll notice dozens of upsells and cross-sell recommendations, all strategically placed and prompted. As a frequent user of their website, I don't find this annoying. Rather, it's valuable to me as a customer because these upsells and cross-sells are positioned and presented in a manner that improves my overall buying experience. When buying a new laptop, I may want to upgrade my battery for a longer life and purchase an additional charging cord to take on the road when I travel to speak at company events.

You likely aren't selling via a website or have any control or influence over your company's website. However, the effort you invest to prepare, position, and present upsells and cross-sells must follow the same approach.

Prepare: Think strategically about:

What upsell and cross-sell offers you can offer
How and when to best present them for the most significant impact
Who you will need support from
When the best time to request a referral will be

Position: Consider the following:

What scripts will you use to introduce upsells, cross-sells, and make referral requests?

Who else should you engage for support?

How will you entice them to support your efforts?

What is the best time to introduce your requests to prospects and customers?

How will you follow up?

Present: Apply your SMF by:

Introducing your scripts and testing their impact

Soliciting feedback on scripts and requests from your customer

Tracking progress for each customer or client

Adjusting scripts and timing for the most significant effect

USE YOUR SMF TO ATTRACT EVEN MORE CUSTOMERS

As we discussed earlier in this book, upsells and cross-sells are a means of ensuring each customer has a positive experience with you and your company. In fact, you are doing every customer or client a disservice if you don't position cross-sells and upsells. You owe it to them to mention these opportunities to improve their overall buying experience, and you limit the chances they'll return disgruntled or upset that something was missing during the sales process.

Good news travels fast, and a properly implemented sales multiplier formula is no exception. When you consider the carefully crafted upsells and cross-sells you'll be sharing with customers at strategic points in the relationship, this will ensure a positive experience. Still, your customers will also be so happy that they want to tell everyone they know. In and of itself, this can provide you with a source of unsolicited referrals and, coupled with the referral system that we designed earlier as part of your sales multiplier formula, can be a source of new business that further multiplies your sales.

Beyond these benefits, your sales multiplier formula will help you craft and position new offers for your customers that differentiate your company amidst a glut of market competition. In other words, when you provide upsell and cross-sell options, you are sharing options and packages with your customers that your competitors likely won't. Sure, they may offer some similar upsell or cross-sell options. However, the method by which you present these at strategic points in the relationship because of your sales multiplier formula will set your offer apart, which can, in turn, increase your chances to stand out and gain even more business.

So, to win the race for new customers in the evolving economy, you must introduce the sales multiplier framework.

TECHNOLOGY IS CHANGING THE SALES GAME (QUICKLY!)

You've likely noticed that I haven't spent much time discussing technology, specifically software, as it relates to your Sales Multiplier Formula, and that's for good reason. Technology in sales, like other areas of our lives, is changing at a rapid pace. New technology is introduced weekly and depending on what you sell and your existing technology, it can aid or hinder your desire to multiply your sales.

I mention "hinder" because I've seen many sales professionals and sales leaders get caught up in technology, forgetting the fundamentals of selling and instead leaning heavily on technology to do all the heavy lifting for them. Unfortunately, this overreliance on technology means that you miss out on the fundamentals of selling, which are to build a relationship of trust which, in turn, allows you the chance to influence decision-making (presuming that what you are selling is both relevant and helpful). In other words, technology can aid your sales efforts, but it won't sell for you.

Considering the different stages of the sales process, it might be helpful to identify technology that can support the various stages of your sales multiplier formula. This list is NOT exhaustive, but rather a summary of software I've used personally, or my clients have incorporated as part of their sales multiplier formula with good results. As with any technology you introduce, however, ensure that the technology assists you (or your sales team) in selling, rather than add additional burdensome steps or unnecessary complexity.

EXAMPLES OF SOFTWARE TO SUPPORT YOUR SALES MULTIPLIER FORMULA

Software to Aid in Your Upsells and Cross-Sells:

Customer Relationship Software to Track the Stage of Each Prospect, Client, or Customer Relationship

When you engage a broader group of employees outside sales to support your introduction of upsells or cross-sells, tracking which customers have engaged can become a challenge. A good CRM software can allow employees to input dates and times upon which your SMF was initiated. Software such as this avoids both duplication of efforts and missed opportunities, and when integrated correctly, it can ensure your sales multiplier formula is applied as you expect. Some examples of CRM software I've personally used include Salesforce, HubSpot, Microsoft Dynamics, Pipeliner, and Zoho, to name a few. The list of CRM software is almost endless, so whatever you choose, ensure you map out your sales multiplier process first and request a demonstration to validate whether the software will support your current process and objectives or not.

You may find CRM software designed specifically for your industry, which is fine. Whatever you do, however, don't fall for the "this software is designed based on industry best practices, so you should change your process to align with the software." Pick what works for you and know that the options are almost endless.

To avoid this, participate in demos to help you understand what changes (if any) will be required in how your sales team operates. If you've introduced a sales system that works, be very cautious about changing it. Just move along to the next software provider. There are plenty to choose from.

Email Automation to Support Making Upsell Recommendations to Prospects

Depending on the CRM software you buy, some will have email capabilities included, meaning that you can email directly from the CRM. Although you may already have a process for doing so, you'll want to consider ensuring the software has email automation capabilities. Often, this is a more complex option you can select. For example, I've used Zoho for some time, and to access the email automation and some other helpful email tools (such as scheduling emails to be sent), I opted to move up from their Professional version to their Enterprise version.

The benefit of email automation is that you can set up automated emails to prospects, customers, and clients. Although the goal is always to personalize communications, you might, for example, schedule a pre-scripted email to be sent to a new customer 30–60 days after their initial buy that asks for input on their experience thus far and provides an incentive for them to make a referral. Another example of email automation might be scheduling scripted emails during the pre-buy phase that appear to come directly from sales and making suggestions on upsell or cross-sell options for the prospect.

If you are using email automation, the key is to avoid overuse, as it can depersonalize the interaction. Consider areas of your sales multiplier formula where communication via email makes sense, and then determine if the email should come directly from someone or if automation is a better option.

Conversation Intelligence Tools (AI) to Make Suggestions on Scripting for Upsells or Cross-Sells

As technology advances, a growing number of conversation intelligence tools can help you make suggestions on ways to improve dialogues with your customers. These tools allow sales calls, over the phone or online, to be recorded for further review and analysis. For example, you may have heard of Chorus from Zoominfo, Outreach, or Gong. Although each of these tools is unique, they all offer the ability to record and provide feedback on sales calls.

In my experience, prospects and customers are okay with using these tools. For example, if you use Chorus during a Zoom call, it will appear that there is an additional participant in your call, which I've found can easily be explained away as your digital note taker (which is what it does). The more significant issue I've encountered is that many sales professionals would prefer this software to listen in on their calls, for various reasons.

I mention conversation intelligence tools because they help ensure that those who don't work in sales but are part of your sales multiplier formula can gain real-time feedback on improving their language. You need to use these tools to be fully confident that those you've engaged as part of your process are doing what they should be.

Other software tools can assist you in launching and managing your sales multiplier formula. However, these are the basics and will provide what you need to ensure you stay on track with your efforts. As mentioned elsewhere in this book, the extent to which you introduce or use these tools will depend on what you sell, the market you sell into, the size and maturity of your company, and several other factors. When it comes to identifying and incorporating software, my motto is simple. Begin with the end in mind. In other words, get your sales process and methods working first, then find software that can aid in the process to improve the speed and quality of your sales results. That's how you ensure technology acts as an aid, not a distraction.

Software to Support Your Referrals

Regarding referrals, the same software listed above can also be an aid. However, there are a few additional considerations, so mentioning them here is essential. There are three rules to generating repeat referrals, aside from selling a great product or delivering an exceptional service. I explain them below.

Shawn's Rules for Generating Repeat Referrals:

Rule #1: You consistently ask for referrals from every prospect and customer you encounter.

Rule #2: You ask with specificity to solicit a direct response (i.e., a yes or no answer).

Rule #3: You track who you asked and when allowing you to follow up as necessary.

To ensure your referral system is fully adopted and applied by everyone, achieving the rules above, there is additional software to consider, as follows:

1. Sales Role Play Software
   Software such as Practis and Second Nature AI can be useful in helping both salespeople and non-salespeople with their language and approach to soliciting referrals.
2. Real-Time Sales Coaching Software
   Providing feedback in real time is an important component of adjusting behaviors. Software like Gong.io and Mindtickle are both resources that capture scripts and language from calls and provide real-time feedback on adjustments to language that can improve results.

3. Sales Engagement Software

   They say timing is everything. Your ability to solicit and receive referrals requires engaging your prospects and customers at the right time, as outlined in the earlier process. Although you can identify the best times to ask for a referral, there is no guarantee that the employee you expect to ask is in the office that day or that the prospect or customer is available that day. Software like Outreach.io and Apollo.io can ensure your timing is on point and consistent.

All the software mentioned above has additional features, so you may find a single solution that will address all your needs. Just heed my earlier warning; decide the gaps in your referral process and then seek out software that can address the gaps. Refrain from getting caught up believing that any of the software listed above will handle soliciting referrals, making upsells or cross-sells for you. They won't.

SALES MULTIPLIER FORMULA 2.0

What happens if you implement the sales multiplier formula and want more? At some point, you'll likely want even more upsells, additional cross-sell opportunities, and an increase in the number of referrals from each customer or client. What changes or adjustments do you need to make to your formula?

Your sales multiplier formula has eight steps that act as a lever, meaning you can make small adjustments to speed up the results of your SMF. Just as these areas can help you increase the number of upsells, cross-sells, and referrals, you can, in most instances, reverse or reduce these adjustments to slow down your new sales opportunities, although I'm not quite sure why you would want to do this.

Seven Steps to Accelerate Your SMF Results

1. Improve Your Positioning: If you'd like to accelerate the sales opportunities, you're your SMF, so you'll need to consider how you can introduce your upsell and cross-sell options sooner and for a more significant impact. How you do this can differ depending on what

you sell. Still, as an example, mention upselling options during initial qualification meetings to increase awareness and entice your prospects to consider these options to influence their overall budget and perception of the value of your offer.

2. Better Follow-Up and Monitoring: When you get better at monitoring where each customer is in their sales journey, you can become more strategic in when and how you make your upsell, cross-sell, and referral requests. For example, you might find that you can offer the upsell or cross-sell earlier with eager prospects or solicit referrals earlier from prospects who show clear signs of willingness to buy.

3. Expand Involvement of Others: Although you may have initially engaged employees you work with who are customer-facing, ask yourself, who else can serve your mission to support multiplying your sales? Can you entice champion customers (those who love you and your product or service) to solicit referrals for you on an ongoing basis? Can you bring these customers into discussions with prospects (in-person or by a pre-recorded video) to increase the willingness and acceptance of buying your upsell or cross-sell options? Remember, the more people you can involve in your SMF, the more selling opportunities you'll have.

4. Increase Upsell Options: Can you position and present other upsell options? Ask your existing customers what would have made their investment better, more appealing, or created the desire to invest sooner in upsells.

5. Increase Cross-Sell Options: Like the steps above, what insights or ideas can you solicit from existing customers to help you improve or increase the number of cross-sell options you provide?

6. Cast a Bigger Referral Net: You can have your existing customers or prospects provide you with referrals. Who else can give you referrals? Think about your professional network, other salespeople selling non-competitive products or services, colleagues at previous companies you've worked with, or other professionals who sell to the same kinds of companies and with whom you can form a referral exchange agreement. Everyone knows someone, so the question is, how can you tap into this and broaden your referral network?

7. Strategic Association Partnerships: Associations with members always look for two things. More members and more ways to serve those members. Are there associations your ideal customers belong

to that you could investigate providing support to in return for exposure to their members? Options can range from giving customers a complimentary service or product to becoming more involved in the association (i.e., joining a committee) to generate relationships from the inside.

You can use other methods to accelerate your sales multiplier framework; however, these are the most straightforward and proven methods.

There is one last thing I'd like to address before I let you go. The greatest threat to success with your sales multiplier framework is losing focus over the long term. So, let's discuss this next.

STAYING FOCUSED OVER THE LONG TERM

Suppose you've taken the steps laid out in earlier chapters. In that case, you have the framework and methods to multiply your sales, generate unsolicited referrals, and even engage other employees in supporting your mission. Over the long term, however, you're going to experience challenges that will threaten to revert you to old habits.

The economy will slow and lessen your sales.

Long-term customers with whom you've built strong relationships will move on to other companies (which you can transition to an opportunity!) or retire from working.

New software and technology will distract your attention from the tried-and-true systems you've built after reading this book.

Even employees you've invested time with to help you generate increased upsells, cross-sells, and referrals may leave your company.

Possibly, your manager will move on, resulting in having a new boss who doesn't fully support your sales multiplier formula.

You might even lose interest in following these steps and decide to pursue a different method. My advice is don't. The key to selling and having success with the sales multiplier formula is that you stick with it over the long term. Jumping from job to job, product to product, or sales system to sales system won't help you to learn from what you apply. Anything you've learned to do well is the result of sticking with it, from riding a bicycle to driving a car, from playing t-ball to playing in the major leagues. When you stick with something, you move from amateur to pro, student to professional.

I suggest sticking with this system, practicing the three Ps, and staying on point. Your results will only improve over time when you continue to improve your sales multiplier formula.

For ongoing resources in support of implementing your sales multiplier formula, make sure to visit www.salesmultiplierformulabook.com.

Sales Multiplier Mindset: Good luck in your journey, and make sure to visit my website for ongoing resources and support to assist you – www.shawncasemore.com.

Index

Pages in *italics* refer to figures and pages in **bold** refer to tables.

Printed in the United States
by Baker & Taylor Publisher Services